THINGS A BAKED ALASKA TAUGHT ME

and other uncommon lessons
from the life of

ELDER DALLAS N. ARCHIBALD

by Linda R. Archibald

THINGS A BAKED ALASKA TAUGHT ME

Distributed by

Granite Publishing and Distribution, L.L.C.
868 North 1430 West • Orem, UT 84057
(801) 229-9023 • Toll Free (800) 574-5779
FAX (801) 229-1924

Production by www.SunriseBooks.com

ISBN: 1-930980-64-7
Library of Congress Control Number: 2001098722

for everyone who loved him—
especially Teresa, Rita, and Helen

"He always had a knack for turning everything into an absolutely wonderful, beautiful thing..."

—Teresa Dawn Archibald, in tribute to her father,
December 28, 1998.

CONTENTS

ACKNOWLEDGMENTS

Because of the countless people who provided assistance and support in December 1998, composing a list of those to whom I am eternally grateful is virtually impossible. The staff at the area offices of the Church in Santiago, the mission presidents and other church leaders in Chile, the members throughout the country, the Chilean search and rescue team all have my undying appreciation.

In addition, prayers were offered around the world—first for Dallas's safety and then, after he had been missing for several days, for a prompt recovery of his body. Those prayers also included petitions for peace and comfort for me, Teresa, and for the rest of the family. I am grateful for those prayers and can testify that those petitions were granted.

When I began trying to compile the material for this book, I thought it might be difficult, emotional. On occasion it was, but generally the research and writing was filled with joyful memories; memories for which I am profoundly grateful.

So many people who knew him and learned from him have willingly shared their personal recollections and thereby helped me refine this material. Again the list is endless.

Jerald and Sharon Taylor and David and Kathy Broadbent kindly spent time—in person and by long distance e-mail—checking the written accounts for accuracy and offering suggestions.

As I began sorting and organizing, sometimes I needed to talk about the material or the format. Thankfully Jean Alder, Luann Day, Kirk Jones, Jane Kennedy and Barbara Marchant listened—and often asked good questions.

Jeanne Hatch willingly supplied exceptional editing expertise.

Cory and Gayle Bangerter read the work and furnished spiritual and ecclesiastical perceptions.

Abigail Tellini studied it, provided a view through Brazilian eyes, and consented to translate it into Portuguese.

And, in free time he didn't really have, Robert Lemon scrutinized the manuscript and returned clear and precise feedback. His assistance gave me specific direction and truly went above and beyond the call of duty.

Finally, I applaud Jeff Lambson at Granite and Brian Carter at SunriseBooks for their professional support and assistance.

I treasure my friends and family wherever they may be. Some of their names appear in this book. To them and to the myriad around the world whose names do not appear but whose association Dallas and I cherish, I send my love.

Teri, I thank you for those "wonderful, beautiful" words.

And to Dallas: "Até logo."

PROLOGUE

Monday; December 14, 1998
Bio Bio River; Santa Barbara, Chile

Summer in the mountains of Chile stirs the soul and bonds it to the beauty and majesty of nature. A country of stark contrasts, Chile stretches north and south for 2,700 miles but barely reaches 110 miles east and west. The Atacama, a desert of incomparable dryness, covers the north. The frigid, windswept south nearly touches the Antarctic. Through the center, innumerable volcanoes—65 listed as still active—dot the landscape. Inactive craters provide peaceful recesses for serene lakes. The Pacific Ocean on the west lures fishermen to it, as do the rivers that flow into it from the towering Andes mountains: Rivers of cool, bubbling water filled with trout—the fish of his childhood.

Elder Dallas N. Archibald, of the First Quorum of the Seventy and president of the Chile Area for the Church of Jesus Christ of Latter-day Saints, was just a fisherman at heart. He identified with those fishermen of the New Testament: Cast your nets…cast your rods…cast your words. He fished for fish and, in the semantics of the gospel, he fished for men. His love of mountain streams and trout had taken root during his childhood and youth in northern Utah. His love of fishing for men had blossomed while, as a young man, he served a mission to Uruguay.

He was a teacher of renown and a powerful motivator. He changed people's lives.

On this Monday morning, he was taking a well-deserved break from church duties after a long weekend of meetings and stake conference sessions with President David K. Broadbent of the Chile Concepción Mission. Monday was almost always P-day (preparation day) and, for Elder Archibald, preparation meant relax, wind down, forget about the clock and the schedule. Whenever possible, seek out a lake or a river and find a few fish. Southern Chile was a paradise for such a fisherman and the Bio Bio River was one of the most spectacular places in the world for an outing.

Elder Archibald and President Broadbent were both expert fishers of rivers. The first had invited the second to accompany him to the Bio Bio for a summer morning. Since mission presidents also need breaks from the intense responsibilities of church duties and are allowed P-days to enjoy recreation of preference with family and friends, President Broadbent accepted the invitation. Early Monday morning, after packing the gear in the car, they drove alongside the river, through pristine mountain scenery, sharing thoughts about the days of work and the days of rest.

The Bio Bio can be a rough river when at its peak but, after two years of drought in Chile, the mountain river, though deep, had been reduced to a calm and rather ordinary flow, meandering lazily through a spectacular wilderness of flat-lands and canyons. The two men felt comfortable with the peaceful river and in awe of the surroundings. Once up-stream they parked, walked to the river's edge, and slipped into float tubes. From there they would leisurely journey to a box canyon where the deep water was still and silent like a lake and there were fish in abundance.

Floating and fishing. The best relaxation in the world. The breathtaking scenery made it even more invigorating. Elder Archibald floated a few yards ahead as they moved on slowly. They were grateful that this morning was bright and sunny. Had it rained today, as it did the day before, they would not have been enjoying the peace and the wonder of the river.

Suddenly they saw the interference, a small area of turbulence where a tributary merged and had, over time, carried a few rocks into the Bio Bio. During their morning drive, that section of the river was hidden from view. Elder Archibald motioned to President Broadbent, indicating that they should shift their trajectory slightly. In response, both float tubes rotated and President Broadbent turned his back to Elder Archibald.

President Broadbent navigated the area successfully in a matter of seconds. He then looked around and was startled to see Elder Archibald swimming, no longer in his fishing float tube. Because a float tube is almost like wearing a piece of clothing and is extremely difficult to remove, he assumed that the float tube must have had some defect. As Elder Archibald angled toward the shoreline he waved, apparently communicating that the two should meet on the river bank around the approaching bend. Then he swam around the bend, out of sight.

President Broadbent rounded the bend a few seconds later expecting to see Elder Archibald waiting for him on the bank, but he was not there. Because so little time had elapsed, he assumed that he had passed Elder Archibald in the river. He climbed out and walked back around the bend. Nothing. He walked up and down the banks of the river calling his name, expecting him to step out from the brush at any time. Still nothing. Twenty minutes later, unable to quell the anxiety churning within him, he began his walk to the nearest road where he flagged down a trucker and soon called the national police and the area office of the Church in Santiago.

By nightfall, despite a massive search effort, Elder Archibald was still missing. His float tube had been recovered intact, with no defect.

The police in Chile issued an all points missing persons' bulletin which was picked up by the wire services and sent around the world on the Internet. By the next morning, the extensive search for the leader of The Church of Jesus Christ of Latter-day Saints in Chile would be a major news story.

That night, from Santiago, I reluctantly called family members in the United States to notify them that Dallas was missing and presumed drowned.

I, however, wasn't ready to give up hope. Dallas had always been a bounce back, beat the odds kind of person. To him life was "a wonderful, beautiful thing"—and he taught me to believe in miracles.

STARTING OUT

July 24, 1938. Logan, Utah. The merry-go-rounds whirled, the children shot cap guns, and townspeople dressed in western outfits milled in front of the booths at the fairgrounds. He had picked a state holiday, the ninety-first anniversary of the Mormon pioneers' entrance into the Salt Lake Valley, as the day to take his first breath of earthly air.

His parents, Ezra Wilson and Marguerite Nielsen Archibald, named him Dallas. In later years when people would ask from whence came his first name, the ever-present comedian in him would relate one of two tall tales. First: "My parents wrote their favorite names on slips of paper and put them in a cowboy hat. My dad held the hat up high and my mother reached up to pick out the name. She got the manufacturer's label." At other times he would use a second silly story: "My parents wanted to name me after that noble city where I was born," he would solemnly proclaim, after which he would pause evoking the inevitable question: "You were born in Dallas, Texas?" "No," he would reply as a grin began to form at the corners of his mouth, "but they didn't feel comfortable naming me after Elizabeth, New Jersey."

Not long after he was born, his parents, with their three sons, settled in Ogden, Utah.

Dallas was a darling baby with curly red hair and then an adorable little boy with an endearing smile and a penchant for mischief. One

1

Sunday morning, he secretly took his pet hamster to church. When the little critter ate right through the pocket of his jacket, Dallas had to make an early and rapid exit from Sunday School.

One day he raced home from school and enthusiastically banged through the back door eagerly calling for "Mom!" The torn shirt and the traces of blood on his upper lip from the "debate" with the boy who called him teacher's pet didn't matter much to him. What did matter was the rolled, smudged paper in his back pocket which dubbed him the Class "D" marble champ of the entire school. His school was as big as the world and he was champion!

Another time he hustled in that same back door with a squirting garden hose in hand. Then he stealthily crept through the kitchen and the living room and finally burst, with water spraying, out the front door—taking his suddenly soaked older brother totally by surprise, and winning the sibling water fight, hands down!

From the beginning, Dallas was a master of adventure and imagination.

When he started school at age six, there were many children in his class with blonde hair and blue eyes. Only one boy, a Native American, had black hair, black eyes, and olive-colored skin. He and Dallas very quickly became good friends and spent as much time together as possible.

At the time Dallas was reading many stories about mountain men, trappers, and Indians; and from *The Book of Mormon* he knew about the Lamanites—King Lamoni and Samuel the Lamanite and their people—and of the promises made to their descendants because their Father in Heaven loved them very much.

One night, Dallas decided that he wanted to become a Lamanite, a Native American, like his friend. He knelt down before going to bed and asked his Father in Heaven to please give him black hair, black eyes, and dark skin. He knew faith could move mountains so he felt that his request should be pretty easy to fulfill.

Early the next morning he awoke excitedly and ran to the bathroom to look in the mirror, anxious to see what had happened during the night. When he saw that his appearance hadn't changed at all, he was discouraged and confused. He couldn't understand why his prayer had not been answered.

Years later, when he told me this story, I realized that his prayer had been answered in a remarkable way. Although the color of Dallas's hair, eyes, and skin didn't change, God worked a little magic in his heart. He gave him the ability to deeply love people of different cultures, races, and languages. That gift would serve him well as he lived in many different countries and was counted as a special friend by many different people.

STABILIZING

As the next few years went by, the boy named Dallas was mellowed and molded by scouting, fishing, hunting, work, education, religion, and the love of understanding parents.

As a teenager, he earned "mad money" in after school hours by working at a corner grocery store. Through hours of daily practice, he won the position of first chair trombone in the Utah all-state band. Civic involvement elected him to the house of representatives at Utah's Boys' State. And, in sports, he was awarded a "letter" in wrestling.

Nighttime provided freedom for his mind and the opportunity to write. A thought-provoking essay composed during one of these contemplative moments won an award in a University of Utah writing contest.

But his first love, always and forever, was fishing. He transformed the weeds in the neighbor's garden into fishing flies and stuck them in the crown of an old, battered forest ranger's hat. Pheasant and peacock feathers dipped from the back of the hat and formed a sweeping tail which fluttered and popped in the wind as Dallas propelled the new motorbike he had purchased from paper route savings toward the mouth of the canyon. The sun tanned his skin, and the depths of the river surrendered the fish—fish that had avoided the experts, only to be fooled by a boy.

On overnight scouting trips, he was never in camp for breakfast. At dawn he went alone with his pole to the lake, and he always brought back enough lunch for everyone.

Butterfly Lake in the high Uintah mountains of Utah was his personal retreat. He loved the constant cool air, the lively trout, and the soft whistle of the wind through the pine trees. Because of his love for pine trees, his parents planted one in his honor in the back yard—and it grew in stature along with him.

On an outing with his father he once asked, wistfully: "Dad, in the celestial kingdom will we be able to go fishing together?" And his father wisely replied, "If it is still important to you, then I'm sure it will be possible."

That conversation laid the foundation for a story Dallas later wrote for *The New Era*.

Staying Afloat
   by Elder Dallas N. Archibald (© by Intellectual Reserve, Inc.; Previously published in *The New Era* magazine; July 1996; 41-44; used by permission.)

The brightest part of the flame of the pine logs had mellowed into glowing coals as Rob stared into the fire. The heat was strong enough to scorch his face and shins, yet the mountain air chilled his back and shoulders. His dad was sitting on a large rock on the other side of the fire, but neither had spoken for some time. Rob was lost in memories of many other times like this and wondering when the next opportunity would come, if ever.

Every year for six years, Rob and his dad had spent at least one week in the summer on a camping and fishing trip. Last year they had boated to the far end of Yellowstone Lake and camped with the bears.

It would have been great to go there again, but Rob wanted to return to the first spot his dad had taken him when he was 12 years old.

As they parked the car and began their hike up the trail, the early morning sky was just beginning to show signs of light. The packs were heavy because of a few extras which would make the camp a little more comfortable. Still, they were experienced enough to know what they could and couldn't do without. The ten-and-a-half mile hike along a cold rushing mountain stream brought them finally to a small lake nestled in a valley cradled at the edge of the timberline of the upper curvature of the mountain.

The natural beauty was breathtaking and the fishing was superb, but as the hypnotic effect of the glowing coals relaxed strained and tired muscles, Rob meditated on the real reason he wanted to come to this spot. At about this same time of night at a similar fire in the same fire pit six years before, he had asked his father, "Dad, in the celestial kingdom will we be able to go fishing together?"

In just a few words of profound wisdom, his father had responded, "If it is still important to you, then I'm sure it will be possible."

Over those six years, Rob had recognized some changes in himself. Although these times with his father continued to be important and he was always ready to go when someone said "fishing," he had learned that fishing was for relaxation and not really a key desire of his heart. In Institute classes during his first year of college, a strengthened testimony of the gospel began burning within him and he knew that as soon as possible after his 19th birthday he needed to be leaving on a mission. The words were clear in his mind and seemed to ring out within his soul: "For how knoweth a man the master whom he has not served, and who...is far from the thoughts and intents of his heart?" (Mosiah 5:13). Nevertheless there were some fears, down deep inside of him, about his ability to do the work.

Time has a way of rearranging priorities. Rob was very aware of that, and sensing the end of an era, he had wanted to come back to this place.

His dad spoke, breaking the silence of the night. "The evening fishing was really something, wasn't it, son?"

"Yeah," responded Rob instantly. "I never believed that I would be catching two fish at a time. But when I tied the second gray hackle yellow on the line, I had to keep my hands inside the float to keep the fish from getting it before the knot was finished. It was like being able to walk on water and get right out there where the fish were biting."

With a slight chuckle, his dad commented. "Now you sound like the apostle Peter. You must have had a lot of faith that those fish were going to give you the thrill of a lifetime."

Rob didn't speak for some time and the still of the night began to inch its way back around the edges of the glow of the campfire which silhouetted the forms of the father and son.

"Dad?" Rob's voice was full of question.

"Yes?"

"Tell me about Peter. How did he walk on water?"

There was a moment of silence before his dad began. "The scriptures say Jesus had sent his disciples ahead of him by ship and he had gone up on a mountain to pray. Apparently the winds were contrary and the water was in high waves. The ship wasn't making much progress. Sometime between three and six o'clock in the morning, Jesus came to them, walking on the sea. Logically they were terrified until Jesus said, 'Be of good cheer; it is I; be not afraid.'

"Then Peter cried out, 'Lord if it be thou, bid me come unto thee on the water.' And Jesus simply replied, 'Come.'

"Rob, this is an important point. When God commands, anything is possible. Remember when Nephi was building the ship and he needed to rebuke his brothers for ridiculing him? He said that if God commanded him to do all things, he could do them. If God commanded him to turn water to earth, he could do it. Miracles are accomplished at the command of the Lord or through the direction of the Holy Ghost. The Savior had said to Peter, 'Come.' At that command, Peter stepped out of the ship and began to walk on the surface of the water as if it were dry ground. But, in fact, it was a storm-tossed sea. Perhaps Peter, who had spent much of his life upon the sea, said to himself, This can't be, and immediately he began to sink.

"The Savior stretched forth his hand, caught him and then said, 'O thou of little faith, wherefore didst thou doubt?' (See Matt. 14:22-33.)

"In the School of the Prophets in the early days of the Church in Kirtland, Ohio, it was taught that where doubt is, faith has no power. The moment Peter doubted the possibility of what was happening to him, his faith lost its power to support him on the water. The scriptures don't say that he had lost his faith in the Lord; so perhaps the doubt was in his own ability.

"Today you were supported in the water by an inner tube full of air and a support system that permitted you to sit there comfortably while you fished. If you had taken a knife and stabbed it into the inner tube, how long would you have stayed afloat?"

"Huh? With all the gear on, I'd sink like a rock. But, Dad, I understand that because a float is like a boat. It's a device made for travel on water. But Peter...How did that work?"

"If you'll get me a pot full of water, I'll give you a demonstration that may help."

In less than a minute, Rob had grabbed the largest cooking pot they had, gone to a small stream by the side of the camp, filled the pot with water, returned to the fire, and placed a few more logs on it to give better light. He knew he was about to receive some special instruction and he was ready.

In the meantime, his dad had placed a piece of steel wool and a small bottle of dishwashing soap on a flat rock near the fire. Rob couldn't resist commenting with a smile, "Dad, we've already washed the dishes."

Letting the one-liner slide by, his father began. "Without proper displacement, like in a ship, steel is not supposed to float. But watch this piece of steel wool as I place it on the surface of the water, in the pot. It floats. You learned the reason why in physics. It is because of surface tension. The pressure of the molecules against one another on the surface of the water will support the steel fibers. If we break the surface tension, watch what happens. Let's add just one small drop of dishwashing soap to the water. The surfactants, chemicals in the soap which break surface tension so dishwashing can be effective, break the surface tension below the steel wool and…look. Rapidly the steel wool now acts like steel should and sinks to the bottom of the pot.

"We don't know if Peter's faith strengthened the force of the surface tension of the water or if it made him lighter, or if some other force was at work. It really doesn't matter. What does matter is that the moment he began to doubt, the miraculous power of faith which permitted him to walk on water was broken and he sank, just like steel wool.

"Faith is not a simple subject, Rob. In general terms, our faith must have four parts. First of all we must have faith in our Heavenly Father, that he loves us and will bless us as we do his will. Then we must have faith in Jesus Christ and that through his atonement we can become clean and pure after proper repentance. How can we have his Spirit to be with us if we are not willing to take his name upon us, remember him always, and keep his commandments?

"Next, we must have faith in our leaders. If we doubt their counsel, it is like knifing our own inner tube or using a surfactant to break the surface tension under our feet. In the gospel, if we doubt the prophet, the General Authorities, or our local leaders, we sink like a rock.

"Last, but not least, we must have faith in ourselves; in our own ability to receive guidance and revelation because we are abiding by the other aspects of faith. As a result, we can receive the assurance that we do know the will of God and are able to carry it out.

"The Savior of all mankind said to Peter, 'Come.' Through the Spirit, it is as if he were saying to you, Rob, 'Come. Trust in me. Serve a mission and I will bless you. Have faith in your Heavenly Father, in me and in the Atonement, in priesthood leaders and in yourself.' When you do these things, then, if the Lord commands, you will have the power to do all things, including walking on water."

Father and son sat quietly for some minutes watching the embers dim. The warmth Rob felt now was not from the fire. It came from within, and he felt sure and strong as the words formed in his mind: "Come. Be not afraid."

STRETCHING,
TEACHING, LEARNING

After high school Dallas enrolled at Weber State University, then simply called Weber College, a small two-year academic institution in Ogden, Utah. Those two years were filled with much outside work, many social activities, and some "part-time" studying. His parents moved from one side of town to the other and he drifted somewhat from church attendance until his new bishop, Keith W. Wilcox, called him in for a little chat.

After some small talk, Bishop Wilcox became serious. Looking him in the eye he asked, "Dallas, have you considered going on a mission?" Dallas gulped. The year was 1958, a time when few young men served missions. The bishop, aware that he had created stunned surprise, simply challenged Dallas to consider leaving in six months.

That afternoon Dallas told his friends about the interview. They started calling him "Elder" and all had a good laugh, all except Dallas. As the day progressed, the novel idea of being Elder Archibald didn't seem to him to be very odd or very funny at all.

Six months later, totally prepared, he received his mission assignment in the mail: "Called to serve in Uruguay." *Where*? He went in search of a map and found Uruguay on the eastern coast of South

America. It was the beginning of a love affair with a continent and a culture.

Because the only language training in those days was accomplished on location, in the mission field, he departed for Uruguay with a repertoire of about a dozen Spanish words. There, in Uruguay, work was the key to happiness and success. Up at six o'clock every morning, shower and shave, eat, study, and then out to the streets to knock on doors and tell the world of a new way of life. He worked twelve to fourteen hours a day. He learned to understand the people. He learned their language and customs. He became one of them.

After a year as a missionary, he was assigned as a branch president to open new areas and establish the Church program. Since he was only twenty years of age with little administrative experience, he learned by trial and error how to set up yearly budgets, train local members to assume positions of responsibility, and then motivate and supervise them in their newly acquired positions.

On his mission he served with members and was never called to be a leader among his peers—never a district leader, zone leader, or assistant to the president—and he wondered if he was unworthy or incapable of handling those responsibilities. He had done his best in all he was asked to do, still the question remained until years later when he was called to be a bishop. Then, as he settled into his office and the duties of his call, he realized he knew exactly what was expected of him and the Spirit confirmed the long-awaited answer: "You received your leadership training through business opportunities. You received your ecclesiastical training on your mission." And he realized that God always knew exactly what he needed.

The two-and-a-half years in Uruguay passed swiftly. Of his departure he wrote: "As the wheels of the plane lifted from Uruguayan soil, I felt an invisible bond that nostalgically tugged and pulled at my emotions. I had been given a challenge. I had met the challenge. I was triumphant. I was Hannibal crossing the Alps. I felt lost. I felt victorious."

In the ensuing decades, that nostalgia was never far away. Any sight, sound, or smell even vaguely reminiscent of Uruguay created in him a sense of euphoria, of happiness and tears.

Because he received vision and spiritual strength from his mission, he would ever encourage young men to serve; for he knew that in the call they, too, could learn to live with faith through love.

The Potter's Hand

by Dallas N. Archibald (© by Intellectual Reserve, Inc.; Previously published in the *Ensign* magazine; October 1990; 17-21; used by permission.)

While serving as a mission president, I often received inspiration enabling me to give appropriate counsel to the missionaries I supervised. During these special moments, images, experiences, and scriptures often leaped into my mind, giving me an understanding not only of the answer to a particular problem, but also of insights into uncommunicated aspects of the problem itself. My relationship with Elder Merrill (not his real name) exemplifies this process.

Once a month, a few days before new missionaries arrived in the field and as those who had finished their time of service were to return home, I met with my two missionary assistants to plan the transfers for that month. After kneeling together to ask for the Lord's help in making these critical decisions, the three of us worked together to appoint new leaders and senior companions and to form new companionships. Most months the procedures went smoothly, although they consumed the better part of a day. Occasionally, however, transfer days progressed to a certain point, then we would find ourselves suddenly confronted with a stupor of thought.

On one such day, the papers on my desk lay in a state of confusion matching the feelings that ran through my mind. Again I reviewed the pictures of the 140 elders and 32 sisters lining the office wall. They seemed to stare back at me in anticipation of the decisions that would affect their lives. However, for the moment the Spirit was not confirming the actions we had planned. After counseling with my assistants, I had to make the final decisions myself. I had asked to be left alone. I analyzed each proposed change, but I could not find peace. Something was wrong.

Suddenly, a knock on my open door dissipated the clouds of my concern, and my eyes focused immediately on the furrowed brow and tightened lips of one of "my" elders. He wore a dark business suit, a white shirt, a conservative tie, and a pair of highly polished but slightly used shoes. At first glance, the attire appeared to be the same as that worn by thousands of others of those chosen to serve in their youth. But I knew this elder was different from most. His suit was not made of the usual polyester fiber, but was woven of costly combed wool. His tie was monogrammed, and his shirt had a matching initial on the pocket. From personal interviews, weekly letters to the president, and other encounters, I knew him quite well.

Usually two or three months is sufficient for adjustment to mission life and foreign culture, but this elder had passed this time without becoming acclimated. Nevertheless, he possessed a youthful testimony and a desire to serve the Lord. His parents—wanting only the best for their only child—had recently written to me of their apprehensions about his happiness, his progress, and his current companion. They had always given him everything he needed and wanted. Now he was in someone else's charge.

I felt a smile widen my face as I greeted him enthusiastically.

"Hello, Elder Merrill."

Even at a distance, his swallow was almost audible.

"President, may I talk with you?"

I rose from my chair and came around my desk, extending my hand. "Of course. Come in and sit down."

He took a seat at the round table in the corner of my office, and I closed the door. As I sat down beside him, I noticed that his normally radiant blue eyes were clouded, as if a veil had been drawn, and there was a trace of redness from tears or lack of sleep.

I waited.

"President, I'm not happy."

I waited again while he twisted his ruby ring two full turns around his finger.

"President, I've tried everything. I've fasted. I've prayed. It just won't work. I don't love the people. They laugh at my Spanish and slam the door in my face. I don't love my companion. He tells me all the things I do wrong. I'm tired of trying. I wonder if I should go home."

I paused a moment, then suggested, "Before discussing such a difficult subject, let's invite the Lord into our conversation."

As we knelt together, he offered a prayer of hope and searching, mixed with doubts. During his prayer, I prayed in my heart for the ability to understand him and for the help of the Spirit to guide me.

After the prayer we exchanged brief testimonies as was our mission custom. His testimony was strong. I knew it would bring him through this crisis. He only needed direction, and I needed to know what to tell him.

"Elder," I began, "tell me about the people."

As he vented the negative feelings built up inside him, I felt the Spirit filling the vacuum in my mind. I probed deeper. "Why doesn't your companion understand you?"

As he spoke, I heard more than the substance of his words and began to understand that, in this new world of a mission, he was unsure of himself. In a secure LDS family and Church environment, he had always achieved and received, but he had never learned to give.

By the time his flood of frustrations was reduced to a trickle, the counsel he needed to receive had organized itself in my mind.

He raised his head and brought his tear-filled eyes up to meet mine. "President," he pleaded, "I don't want to go home. Please, President, teach me how to love!"

His lower lip began to quiver, and the tears streamed down his cheeks.

Despite the emotion of the moment, I rejoiced inside. He was humble, teachable, willing to serve. My heart went out to him as it had before to so many of these remarkable young elders and sisters. They wanted to be righteous and obedient, yet they struggled with personal weaknesses and challenges. I often thought of the scripture in Ether 12:27 and how it applied to missionaries in particular: "And if men come unto me I will show unto them their weakness. I give unto men weakness that they may be humble." They had come to serve the Lord in His mission field, and there He would show them their weakness to make them humble. I had seen it happen over and over—elders and sisters brought to their knees through personal trials, their testimonies strengthened by the Lord, and eventually their success as missionaries significantly increased.

I looked at Elder Merrill. He was a candidate for such success. The clay had been kneaded and prepared. Now the Potter's Hand was beginning to mold another vessel. As an instrument, called and representing that Power, I paused as he regained his composure. Then I began.

"Elder Merrill, your desires are commendable, for to truly love is the greatest of all attributes. To love unconditionally is to love as our Heavenly Father and His Son love us. The prophet Mormon understood this when he said that the pure love of Christ—which he called charity—is the greatest of all, for all other things must end, but charity endures forever. Charity requires interaction with others—sincere caring and concern, giving of ourselves for the benefit of someone else. Paul talked of this in 1 Corinthians 13:4-8: 'Charity is kind...thinketh no evil...rejoiceth in the truth...beareth all things, believeth all things, hopeth all things, endureth all things. Charity never faileth.' Elder Merrill, let's read these scriptures together."

As he read and marked these verses in his Bible and similar ones in the Book of Mormon, I mentally coordinated the next portion of our discussion. When he had finished, I summarized:

"Can you see from these scriptures that learning to love in the way our Father in Heaven wants us to love is a very important but very complex task?"

He nodded.

"Then we must find a way to begin—a way to take the first step toward acquiring the pure love of Christ. If you properly apply this principle of charity in your life each day, I promise that with the help of the Lord, you will learn to love as you desire." I opened my Bible. "The key is found in 2 Corinthians, chapter 2, verse 2, where Paul says, "For if I make you sorry, who is he then that maketh me glad, but the same which is made sorry by me."

"Now, since his words may seem difficult to understand, I'm writing a translation in today's terminology here on this paper. Will you please read it?"

Elder Merrill took the page from me and read: "If I don't reinforce the good in you, who will reinforce the good in me?"

"Do you understand how positive reinforcement works?" I asked.

He nodded. "It means to tell others of their good qualities."

"Exactly. By using positive reinforcement, two things happen. The first is obvious: We make others feel important and capable. But the second is a miracle. By reinforcing the good in others, we learn to love them because we begin to see their glorious potential. Just as the old adage says, 'To have a friend, you must be a friend.' We must realize that giving comes before receiving. We cannot sit and wait for love to grow. We must do the planting, watering, and tending. Elder Merrill, there are two things you must do to take the first step toward charity." I handed him a pen so he could write them on the page below the words about reinforcement. "One: look for positive actions, attitudes, and abilities in others. Two: Compliment others sincerely and honestly."

When he had finished writing, I asked, "Do you have any questions about these two keys?"

He glanced at his writing and gave a slow shake of his head.

"Can you apply them in your daily life, Elder?"

His reply was guarded. "I think so, President."

"Elder Merrill, I know that you can. Let me give you some examples. If love does not exist between you and your companion, then let it begin with you. Use the keys. Look for his positive traits. Openly and sincerely compliment him. Very soon you will love him because of all the good you have found in him. And when he realizes that he is important and capable in your eyes, he will love you.

"These keys of positive reinforcement can also be used with the people you teach as a missionary. Although we may have difficulty with some of the actions and attitudes of those we meet, the gospel we teach will help them change if we can only create an atmosphere that will allow us to present our message in love.

"For example, upon entering the home of someone of a different faith and observing the presence of religious objects, we might have a tendency to attack those objects and the beliefs they represent. By doing so, however, we force the other person to defend his own importance and capability. This does not create a receptive atmosphere. Instead of criticizing, we must look for positive traits that person has and then reinforce them.

"Let's say you enter the home of Señor Garcia. You might say: 'Señor Garcia, I'm happy to see that you have a belief in our Savior and are active in that belief. Tell me, what does this religious object mean to you?'

"As Señor Garcia talks, listen for the positive points of his faith that match the message you want to teach. Then relay these ideas back to him with sincere praise. As you do so, you will find that you understand him and recognize his worth. He in turn will realize that he is important. In this way, you create an atmosphere of love and respect that will lead you easily into your discussion:

"'Señor Garcia, I'm glad your faith has brought you to this point because now, more than at any other time in your life, you are ready to understand an even greater message that God has prepared for you. In the year 1820, a young boy of fourteen was searching for the truth...'

"Remember, criticism reinforces the negative and destroys feelings of importance and capability. Criticism is not charitable. Trying to teach in an atmosphere of criticism will not nurture love; positive reinforcement will.

"Now, Elder, let me ask again. Can you apply these keys?"

He was silent a moment before I saw the dawning of a smile. "Yes, President," he said firmly. "I can."

We quickly established a follow-up system to measure his progress by using his weekly report to me and occasional personal interviews. He stood up and extended his hand. His handshake was strong, his smile enthusiastic. He left the office with an air of determination.

In contrast with his forcefulness, I closed the door gently to avoid any sudden movement that might destroy the fragile feeling of warmth in the room. After a brief moment of thanks to Him who had provided me with words and direction, I returned to my desk and the transfer board.

21

The pictures on the wall looked back at me again, and my heart surged as the Spirit confirmed what needed to be done. Elder Merrill was the answer. He had been scheduled for a transfer, but he could not be transferred now. He couldn't leave his current companion until he had learned to love him.

Then, as if a high-speed movie were running through my mind, I envisioned the rest of his mission. In accordance with his righteous growth, he would next be called to serve as companion to an elder laboring as a branch president in a new area. Through application of the principles we had discussed, he would learn to love his companions, the members, and the investigators; he would lift and inspire them. He was blessed with the ability to lead his peers, and I knew he would serve where his special brand of love could best be used. He would labor among new members and finish his mission as a branch president.

The months passed. Once again Elder Merrill sat beside me—this time for the final interview of his mission. The costly wool suit was now shiny with wear, and the inside lining sagged from many cleanings. Although the shoes were recently shined, the heels were almost gone, and open cracks in the leather witnessed the many hours he had spent tracting. Branch President Merrill, now a seasoned priesthood leader, had finished his call.

The sparkling blue of his confident eyes seemed even more penetrating, but once again they rimmed with tears. This time, however, his words and feelings were different.

"Tomorrow night I'll be with my parents. I'm excited to see them again. I love them very much. But President, how can I leave this work and these people, whom I also love very much?"

As we both struggled to control our emotions, I gave silent thanks for the gift of inspiration. Through it, the Potter's Hand can mold the clay of our lives into one of His own vessels.

Peter Pan and Wendy

I first saw Dallas on a Sunday morning in March 1961. He had returned home to Ogden, Utah that week from his mission in Uruguay and so he was seated on the stand for Sunday meetings. My family had moved into his ward while he was away.

That moment when I first saw him is frozen in time, maybe because I was a college freshman interested in any returned missionary or maybe because, even though I didn't know it then, it was the beginning of forever.

Three weeks after that first sighting at church, he showed up at my door one Sunday afternoon, unannounced. When the doorbell rang, there was no logical way for me to know who was calling; yet, in the instant before I opened the door, I did know that he was on the other side. He asked, with quiet effervescence, if I would attend a piano concert with him on Tuesday night. I, of course, accepted.

We arrived at the concert by virtue of his brother's ancient Ford coupe, which literally hobbled there and home again. But for him, every chug and jerk warranted a chuckle not a concern. The concert was a professional, sedate, and serious affair which we giggled all the way through because he didn't seem to think it should be sedate and serious. I was concerned about that; but, since it was a first date, I played along. As a result, by the time the evening ended, "proper, responsible, analytical me" was totally captivated by "carefree, sponta-neous, fun-loving him." He was a happy-go-lucky, high-flying "Peter Pan." I was a methodical and reserved "Wendy." I guess we were a per-fect example that opposites attract.

For the next four months we dated constantly: picnics, church dances, group socials, and a string of sacrament meetings where he spoke about his mission. During those latter occasions, he left his play-ful nature outside. The gospel was a serious subject, and he would never trivialize it. His talks were inspiring, and his ability to capture the attention of an audience from the pulpit was a gift which would only improve over time. In those moments he spoke of healings, of conver-sions, of the power of the gospel and the Spirit in people's lives. His joy in missionary work radiated as he quoted his favorite scripture:

"Oh that I were an angel, and could have the wish of mine heart, that I might go forth and speak with the trump of God, with a voice to shake the earth, and cry repentance unto every people!

"Yea, I would declare unto every soul, as with the voice of thunder, repentance and the plan of redemption, that they should repent and come unto our God, that there might not be more sorrow upon all the face of the earth.

"But behold, I am a man, and do sin in my wish; for I ought to be content with the things which the Lord hath allotted unto me" (Alma 29:1-3).

The desire of Alma's heart was to teach truth worldwide with power. Dallas believed that because Alma did the work allotted to him with fervor while on earth, he was granted his heart's desires. Alma now forcefully teaches truth around the world through his words in *The Book of Mormon*.

Although Dallas was a Peter Pan, he was also an Alma; and I was impressed with his sincerity.

While we were dating, the bishop of our ward asked Dallas to organize a youth choir which he did with great gusto. The little group grew rather quickly into a large chorus that had as many socials as rehearsals. He had tremendous rapport with youth which allowed him to persuade them to do many good things, and they even thought it was of their own free will and choice. I joined him in this endeavor as a kind of secretary/organizer (the beginning of my eternal role), and the choir became our summer focal point. Dallas, with tongue in cheek, named them the *FWYCs*, an acronym pronounced "Fweaks," derived from their official designation: Fiftieth Ward Youth Choir.

He inspired them. He motivated them. And he wrote the music and the words they sang.

We will go—and do the things our Father hath commanded.
We will go—and do the things our Father hath commanded.
For we know He gives no law to men,
Save He shall prepare a way for them
To fulfill the things He hath commanded,
For our Father knows our every need.

We will go—and do the things our Father hath commanded.
We will go—and do the things our Father hath commanded.
As God's children we must seek His light,
And beware of Satan's evil fight.
But we're agents over our own actions,
And God gives us as our hearts desire.

We will go—and do the things our Father hath commanded.
We will go—and do the things our Father hath commanded.

As we do the things of righteousness
God is obligated to bless us.
And we'll walk in the path of His glory
And we'll know the everlasting truth.

****

For many years I strayed
    in youthful fantasy,
With testimony weak
    I did not pray to thee.
But still thy loving hand
    did guide me through the years.
Dear Lord, please hear my prayer
    I offer thee in tears.

Dear Lord, this is my prayer
    that I may always live
The way that thou desires,
    and glory to thee give.
The Spirit touched my soul,
    The truth made known to me.
Through study, work, and prayer
    I give my life to thee.

He wrote with sincere simplicity; and the youth sang the same way.

Three months after our excursion to the piano concert, he spontaneously stopped me in my tracks as we were walking quickly through
a jewelry section of a department store. He pulled me toward a cabinet
of diamond rings and nonchalantly asked with a mischievous grin,
"Which one do you like best?" After a brief moment of superficial

evaluation, I laughingly selected one. Fortunately, I really did like it because he simply made the purchase (on time payments) then and there. I was so startled by this sudden turn of events, however, that my cautious, deliberate nature suggested we just keep those rings in layaway for awhile. I had to be sure about this decision. Considering the differences in our personalities, I wasn't certain that we could live happily ever after.

That was the summer of 1961, the summer Russia built a wall to separate East and West Berlin. War talk was in the air and the military draft was still operative. Dallas had a military deferment for his mission and school, but the deferment was temporarily suspended because he was working during the summer to accumulate funds for a return to classes in the fall. When he called the draft board, he was told that his draft notice would be in the mail within three days.

Feeling strongly that he did not want to be a draftee in the Army, did not want to be designated for assignment in Europe at this point in time, he began a rapid but focused canvass of the other possibilities: enlistment in the Army, Navy, Marines, or Air Force. After two days of interviewing, he still had no idea what he should do. Confused, he mentioned his dilemma to a friend who suggested, "Have you considered the Coast Guard?" This was a novel idea that sounded most interesting. Quickly he caught a bus to Salt Lake City (the option at that moment being his brother's ancient Ford) and an interview with the USCG. Afterwards, he returned home with favorable feelings about that meeting but still unsure of the correct route to take, and time was running out. In order to nullify the draft notice, he had to be officially connected to another military option before the papers arrived.

In his room alone, he knelt by his bed. "Father, I have investigated all the options. I feel most comfortable with the Coast Guard. Should I enlist?" The answer, positive, overwhelming, stopped his prayer and took his breath away leaving no doubt about the route he would follow.

The next day he returned his draft notice with his Coast Guard enlistment attached.

He left for Base Alameda near Oakland, California three days later—with those diamond rings still in lay-away.

Considering that this military obligation put his definite plans for education and his indefinite plans for marriage on hold, he remained in remarkably good humor. But then "Peter Pan" has never been known to wallow in depression. He just takes on the next challenge with bravado and enthusiasm.

My life settled into a routine of college classes, afternoon work at a nursery school and, since phone calls were very expensive in those days, writing letters to Dallas.

Then in September, for probably the first and last time in history, the Coast Guard Recruit Band from Base Alameda was invited to perform at the Utah State Fair; and Dallas, by virtue of being an accomplished trombone player, was a member of that band. In eager anticipation of his arrival I bought a new suit (and a new raincoat to accommodate the expected September showers) and went to the fair feeling like someone out of a Broadway musical.

Dressed in Navy Blues he looked dashing, in that special military way, and when our eyes found each other, my heart skipped a beat. I had been thinking of those rings in lay-away for a couple of months, and I wondered where these few days together would take us. He wondered the same thing and the ball was in my court, so to speak, as I had been the one with my foot on the brakes. But no more. I had decided I needed this particular Peter Pan and time would never alter those feelings.

We talked late into that night and, somewhere along the way, the engagement ring ended up on my finger. The next day between band performances we took a quiet, romantic, autumn walk in a light drizzle of rain through the tree-lined pathways of Salt Lake City's Memory

Grove park. When he flew away from Utah thirty-six hours later, we were planning a June wedding and my parents were reeling under the news that I would possess a marriage license before a bachelor's degree.

After completing recruit training, Dallas was asked to remain for a six-month tour of duty with the band and, in his non-musical hours, to work for the captain of the base as secretary of welfare. In this latter responsibility, Dallas was often involved in helping to assist his associates who had financial problems. As a result, he began to get "cold feet" about marriage because we obviously did not have enough money to make ends meet. Even in those "olden" days, $99 a month just wouldn't suffice. He figured and re-figured and prayed and figured again. No matter what kind of adaptations he tried, the funds never stretched far enough. Nevertheless, the Spirit continued to chant: "Get married. Get married. Get married." When Dallas finally confided his concerns to me, he didn't say a word about waiting or wondering. He only said he didn't know how we could do it but, if the Spirit said "GO," there would be a way.

Either we were too young, too oblivious, or too imbued with simple faith to worry about the troublesome possibilities. We even wrote schmaltzy stuff to each other:

To Dallas: Love's Special Season.

No words can say how much you mean to me.
You're in my every thought and dream, it's true.
Now forever happy I will be
For always you'll love me and I'll love you.

That day of April love began our song
Then soon September brought romantic rain;

29

And hand in hand two lovers walked along
Through colored autumn leaves down memory lane.

We've always been together though apart.
You're with me every hour of the day.
I hold a prayer for you within my heart,
And we'll go on with God to light the way.

Then soon together we will always be—
When sealed for time and all eternity.

****

U.S. Coast Guard Base
May 1, 1962

My Darling,

Today is one of those days. It isn't autumn and it isn't raining, but it might just as well be as far as I am concerned. I am in another one of those dazes which carries me far from recognition of my present status and envelopes me in the fluffy swirls of cloud number nine.

In this letter, I have no purpose to accomplish except to try and express as well as possible on paper how much I love you and how much I long for us to be together again. So for now, I'll just dream and write.

When I think of how short the amount of time is that we have left to wait until we will be able to kneel at the altar together, my breath seems hard to find and a burning of anticipation swells up within me. With senses clear and imagination augmented by intellect, an over-powering emotion keeps saying to me that all I have to do is close my eyes and I'll be there.

The paper has turned to velvet beneath the weight of my fingers and the warmth of your hand is near. I have been in those rooms many times before, and they have always given me a strange, mysterious feeling—a feeling such as one would encounter on a moonlit winter night—a feeling that is of hallowed, untouchable beauty.

Now as I ponder on these things, the setting of the room is changed. The hallowed beauty of the House of the Lord as I have remembered it is not changed, but a feeling of warm tear-filled happiness has entered in. I see you and me kneeling there hand in hand across the altar entering into the beginning of the greatest commandment that God has given to his children.

This is the thought that for me turns the snows of winter into crystal so that they may remain even more beautiful while flooded with the warmth of summer sun.

Linda: you have given me great happiness and purpose and I love you very much. You are in my every prayer and I do sincerely pray for the Lord's blessings upon you and our love.

Dallas

I believe this is the only message I ever received from him that was not inundated with humor.

He came home, by bus, for a few days at Thanksgiving and for almost two weeks at Christmas. That was supposed to be all the reunions for us until June, but we couldn't stay apart that long. In March, he somehow squeezed out enough funds for a late-night plane ticket and flew to Utah for a long, but not long enough, weekend.

We set the wedding date for June 8; then, just before the invitations went to press, Dallas called to say the Coast Guard wouldn't let him leave until the following week. We changed the date to June 14 and he rolled into town a couple of days before. Those long spaces of separation always gave my heart a chance to hop, skip, and jump when I saw him. But this time when he left, I wouldn't have to say another good-bye. Gratefully, I would finally be leaving with him.

And so it was that I traded the editorship of the college newspaper and a university diploma for that suddenly selected set of diamond rings. We were married on June 14, 1962: Dallas Nielsen Archibald and Linda Ritchie, husband and wife. A small group of friends and relatives accompanied us to the Salt Lake Temple that morning to see us united for time and eternity. I cried and Dallas snickered at me as a kindly full-time temple sealer, Burtis F. Robbins, gave us personal instructions and guided us through the ceremony.

That evening we had an "open house" at my parent's home, an event that was more like a party than a reception, with Dallas and me trying to stay in one place and greet the line of guests, our parents wandering about visiting with whomever they chose, and kind friends and relatives collecting gifts and serving cake and ice cream. The evening was relaxed, informal, and untraditional, a prelude to the symphony of our life together.

As soon as we could courteously depart from our reception/party, we exited and checked into a hotel in Ogden where they gave discounts to newlyweds. We sorted our gifts over the next three days and packed our 1959 Plymouth (provided by my father for a small down payment with the balance due eventually) for the journey to California. With the business concluded in Utah, the car packed, and the remainder of our belongings stored in the basements of accommodating parents, we left—finally alone. But we could not afford the traditional honeymoon getaways of Honolulu, Niagara Falls, or even Reno. We took two days and one night to get to California. Appropriately, we spent that one night in Lovelock, Nevada—and then went on, straight through Reno, to our new residence in Oakland.

Life began inconspicuously for us in a small studio apartment that had a greasy kitchen, a leaky bathroom, and a broken window and a bed in the wall in the living room. Dallas had warned me about the place, but I was either too young, too oblivious, or too much in love to care. Besides, it was only $65 a month. That left $34 for groceries, gas, and tithing. Fortunately, a small marriage allowance was added to the paycheck just a few weeks later. Nevertheless, until I found work at an Oakland bank and Dallas received a small raise, we learned how to live on very little. But no matter where we were or how much we had (or didn't have), he made sure that life was a laughing matter.

I remember once when we were driving from California to Utah for Christmas in our 1959 blue Plymouth sedan, having scrimped to save the necessary funds for gas. Somewhere near the mighty metropolis of Winnemucca, Nevada he anchored a can of root beer to the front bumper for about thirty long, cold miles in order to turn it frosty. A half-an-hour later, mission accomplished, he retrieved it from the bumper, returned to the warm interior of the car, and popped the cap only to spray brown fizz all over the upholstery. I groaned. He laughed.

Back home in our apartment, one night I burned my tongue on a sip of scorching hot chocolate. He, with all deliberate speed, grabbed a tray of ice from the freezer and thrust it in my direction. My tongue adhered to it as though it had been coated with super glue. He laughed. I panicked.

Even though I got used to having a sense of humor always hanging around, I remained "Wendy"—naturally practical, serious, and organized. In a way, I had no choice. Someone had to "sew his shadow back on" every time he misplaced it, keep any "lost boys" from being lost for very long, and remind him when playtime was over. The job was easy though. He was a Peter Pan with conscience and commitment. Additionally, he didn't require that his Wendy be anyone else. I was blessed to have a companion who accepted me as I was yet encouraged me to reach for the stars.

Sister Marjorie P. Hinckley said of her husband, President Gordon B. Hinckley, "Gordon always let me do my own thing. He never insisted that I do anything his way, or *any* way, for that matter. From the very beginning he gave me space and let me fly" (*Go Forward With Faith, the Biography of Gordon B. Hinckley*; Sheri L. Dew; Deseret Book Co.; Salt Lake City, Utah; 1996; 141).

Because Dallas gave me space and let me fly, I eventually learned how to lock into his coordinates: *"First star to the right and straight on 'til morning!"*

Hearts and Flowers

We had a perfect marriage. We were very good at tolerating, or ignoring, each other's idiosyncrasies. At least he was good at it. And I learned.

Marriage, in my imagination, was cozy togetherness—a romantic fantasy land where we would curl up by the fire together and quietly share affection and philosophy. Perhaps this idyllic vision actually exists in some remote corner of the universe, but it did not exist in mine. Dallas was a mover and a shaker, always hurrying somewhere. He just couldn't slow down long enough for hearts and flowers and candlelight. He had a multitude of ways to turn most sentimental occasions into something slightly silly. He liked to joke and tease and poke, punch, and pinch—while I yearned for a methodical hug or a kiss. I had to learn to accept the fact that everything from playtime to romance would always be infused with a sense of humor.

Because I had expectations of hearts and flowers and didn't often get them, I could have decided that we were incompatible; and he could have assumed we were incompatible because I didn't appreciate his jovial approach. Being new at this kind of relationship, we were not very good communicators in those days so we never discussed our differing perspectives in any detail. I assumed he didn't understand romance. He assumed I was just being stubborn. The main contrast in our response to these perspectives, however, was that he never considered any of this to be a serious problem because, to him, marriage was just liking each other and working things out. I, on the other hand, developed a heavy chip on my shoulder because of the lack of candlelight.

It is true that men and women often approach life, communication, sharing, and togetherness differently. It is also true that different types of personalities have different methods. For example: there are "hurry-hurry" people as opposed to those who believe that "caution is the better part of valor." Add to those differences the reality that some people are structured left-brain dominant types while others are creative right-brain dominant types, that some people are verbal while others are not, some are mathematical while others are not, some are musical while others are not, some are social and some are hermits, some have academic genius and others have athletic genius, some like peace and quiet while others like noise, and on and on and on, ad infinitum.

Considering the array of different combinations possible, it is a wonder that any communication is ever precise enough, compassionate enough, to generate understanding. And without practicing compassionate communication—learning to explain our perspectives and needs to each other—relationships suffer. As a prime example, I offer the story of my joyously anticipated birthday dinner at The Cliff House.

We had saved up for several months, and I had waited anxiously. My birthday present was to be a rare romantic dinner for two at The Cliff House on San Francisco's Pacific Coast. He wore a business suit and I dressed in my little used but lovely white suit with fur collar.

I was so excited. Dinner out—in San Francisco—on the coast—just the two of us. I was savoring every single romantic second, even as I added jewelry to my outfit, because I knew such an occasion would not happen again for a long, long time.

I knew I was radiant, glowing, as we got in the car and drove away. Rounding the corner and passing in front of the apartment of good friends, Dallas said in jovial, spontaneous tones: "Hey, Dawn and Clark got a new dog. Let's stop for a minute."

I paused. The radiant moment in time hit a bump and the light dimmed slightly.

"Now?" I questioned.

"Sure, why not?"

"Well, because…"

"Oh, come on. We'll just be a minute."

He pulled to the curb and parked.

Unsure of what was real at this point and trying to regenerate the light, I suggested, "Just go on in. I'll wait here."

"Are you sure?"

"Yes, I'm sure."

So off he went, returning a couple of minutes later.

"Come on in, just for a second. It's such a cute dog."

I could tell there was no point in resisting. With a sigh I got out of the car and followed him inside and up the stairs to the apartment, silently grumbling all the way.

He opened the door and motioned me to go ahead of him, which I did. There inside, much to my dismay, was the entire group of young married couples from the ward bellowing "SURPRISE," and all waving balloons at me.

As the air slowly escaped from my "opportunity for a romantic evening balloon," my stunned disappointment was evident. I gulped and tried, with very little success, to hide my feelings. As they all gathered around me I attempted to respond graciously to their kindness, but it just wouldn't work. The blow was too great. My act was transparent. I needed to re-group.

" I think," I stammered, "that I'm a little over-dressed. I'll be back in a few minutes."

I left, with Dallas on my heels fuming. "After all the work they went to, the least you could do is be considerate and show a little gratitude!"

How could I explain the hollowness I felt inside. How would he, "Mr. Life of the Party," understand that I was watching romantic moments I had treasured in vision turn to ashes? All I could manage was a very weak, "I'm sorry."

Back home I changed to casual, put the jewelry back in the box, and washed off my makeup. I wasn't happy, but I was now in the right costume. Although I did everything in my power to exhibit joy and appreciation for the evening, I was never a very good actress.

Dallas and I never went to The Cliff House and, at the time, we did not discuss the evening further.

But time heals all wounds and teaches profound lessons. In retrospect, I know what I should have done that night. As the air leaked out of my romantic balloon, I should have first looked at my options for the evening. Since there were no kind, compassionate options, I should have drawn a happy smile on my mouth and on my heart. Then I should have conjured up my best assertive communication. Right after the resounding rendition of "SURPRISE," I should have turned to my eternal companion, winked at him in acceptance of the circumstances, and then sweetly hissed through clenched teeth: "Okay buster, I'll do this with effervescent enthusiasm—but you owe me a dinner, maybe two, and soon!"

In truth, however, if we had been that good at communication I wouldn't have had to take the initiative. As he opened the door at the top of the stairs, he would have slowed our entrance just a tad and whispered in my ear: "Smile, you're on Candid Camera. We'll do dinner next week. I promise." And I would have known he meant it.

On that night, however, we weren't wise enough to communicate effectively, lacking understanding of each other's needs.

About thirty years later, when we had built better bridges of communication and learned to value our similarities and differences, one day he came to me.

"Do you remember the night in California when we didn't go to The Cliff House?"

I felt like exclaiming adamantly, "*I certainly do!*" But I only uttered an unemotional "Yes."

"Well," he hesitated, "I never understood how much it meant to you. I'm sorry."

And I understood that he never understood because I never really told him. Through the years, I could have had many more hearts and flowers if I had not been so reluctant to talk about my needs. Dallas was not adverse to occasional candlelight and curling up by cozy fires. He just didn't see such things as important enterprises until he realized they were important to me. Because I expected him to be able to read my mind and thereby bring resolution to my expectations, it took decades before he understood my desire for a romantic evening at The Cliff House. Since he was quite content with life no matter how it came packaged, I was the one who needed to be able to express my wishes with better compassionate communication.

Sometimes two people who live together in love only learn to communicate effectively over time.

In time we developed a permanently perfect relationship: we were very good at tolerating, or ignoring, each other's idiosyncrasies. He was always good at it, and I learned.

THE MILITARY
MUSIC MAN

A couple of months after we were married and settled in Oakland, Dallas was named director of the Base Alameda Coast Guard recruit band. This was an amazing turn of events given that this assignment traditionally went to a commissioned officer rather than to a lowly enlisted man. Without doubt, there was more than sheer luck involved in the opportunity. We were certain this was at least one reason why Dallas was inspired so forcefully to join the Coast Guard. During his four-year enlistment, his only sea duty would be one trip across San Francisco Bay with the band to perform for a special ceremony.

He immediately began to use his simple musical focus and profound motivational skills to turn a young, transient group of recruits into an award-winning musical unit. Because they were recruits, he could demand near-perfection of them on the march; and because their time and abilities were limited, he had them learn only two march numbers: *The Washington Post March*, and the Coast Guard song, *Semper Paratus*. Though their repertoire was small, they could play those two numbers like professionals. In a parade, they sounded like the Philharmonic on the move.

Because the group was composed of recruits, a few came and went each week; so, with the exception of a dozen or so above average musicians who were asked to remain six months at the base to form a nucleus for the band, there was a complete turnover of personnel every nine weeks. This constantly evolving unit was in competition with professional military bands from well-known military bases all over the West coast.

Within a few months of Dallas's installation as director, the previously insignificant recruit band from Base Alameda began winning first place awards in every parade. As the number of trophies in the display case at the administration building grew, so did Dallas's fame. He was so good at convincing people that the sky is the limit and finding ways to help them reach that high. The director of the rifle honor guard, Mr. Ischaar, caught the spark of enthusiasm from Dallas, and his group soon began bringing home first place trophies in their division.

Even with the growing awards "fever," however, the atmosphere among the troops was relaxed and appreciative rather than being stressful and competitive—another principle Dallas seemed to be able to convey. Though they reveled in the euphoria which resulted from solidly defeating the professionals, the experience was more of a game than a power struggle. They loved the joy of parading and the camaraderie. Winning was a bonus.

When Lynn Crisler, a tall and lanky all-American drum major with crowd-pleasing showmanship, joined the Coast Guard at Base Alameda, Dallas saw a chance to create a little extra pizzazz. With Cris, he choreographed a march routine for the band to use as they passed the reviewing stands.

Before a parade began, Dallas would mark off a certain number of yards ahead of the judging area. Then, as the band approached, he would stand at that location so Cris could identify the exact spot to begin the routine. Cris, who was six-and-a-half feet in height, carried a shiny six-foot mace and a silver whistle. When he could see Dallas out of the corner of his eye, a shrill blast from his whistle and a twirl of his mace propelled the band, like mechanical soldiers, from a four-line marching formation into two lines with every move synchronized, every step identical. Directly in front of the reviewing stand, the music crescendoed and then abruptly stopped. The band turned a quarter of a turn in perfect military precision to face the judges. Not an eye blinked. Not an instrument moved. Seconds passed. 1-2-3-4-5. Cris sounded the whistle again. The two rows of military robots made the quarter turn back to a "Forward! March!" position.

Cris then "hid" himself between the two lines, crouched down, almost out of sight. A blast from his whistle ignited music and march step in the same instant. Ten beats later, on a designated note, the band separated precisely back into four lines and Cris rocketed from his internal position to the forefront of the band, his head thrown back, his six-foot mace high in the air beating the rhythm. The robotic precision, the inspiring music, the heart stopping showmanship always brought "oooo-aaahs" from the crowd. And this enchantment was enhanced by twelve-year-old Ramona Winter, a baton twirling champion, who led out and kept Cris company.

Every little village in northern California seemed to have a parade of some kind at one time or another. I loved traveling with the band on weekends as well as to the week-long summer Seafair celebration in Seattle. For this latter occasion, Dallas flew with the band by military transport and I traveled as cheaply as possible, by Greyhound bus. Most of the band and honor guard members were my age, Dallas only three or four years older. Though Dallas was in charge, and a pretty tough taskmaster at that, we were all friends—kind of like a college crowd in uniform.

At the Coast Guard base, Dallas was also the group leader for LDS servicemen. Meetings were held every Wednesday evening and investigators who were curious about this extraordinary band director would often attend, and sooner or later there would be a baptism.

As Dallas's four years of active Coast Guard duty neared the end, he was pressured from all sides to re-enlist. The military leadership tried to assure him he could remain at Base Alameda forever. The offer was tempting: security, stability, and plenty of honor. We talked and talked about the pros and the cons but, in the end, we declined. We mused that future leaders might decide Dallas needed sea duty or a lighthouse assignment instead of just working musical magic. Mostly, however, with every prayerful request for direction the Spirit seemed to whisper that the military was not to be the road for our future.

So we began the process of disengaging and packing for a return to Utah and university studies, but not until we had made our last trip to Seattle for a glorious week at Seafair. For this finale, we drove north together.

All the Coast Guard musicians and marchers were in high spirits as the festivities began, and the joy and excitement heightened as, day after day, the Coast Guard brought home first place awards. In the previous three years at Seafair, the only parade in which the band had not won a first place trophy was the Chinese District Parade. Tension and hopes were high as we boarded the bus on Thursday night for that parade. The men were poised and at their best. Their performance was flawless.

When the parade ended, everyone milled about anxiously awaiting the judges' announcement of the winners. When every Coast Guard unit took a first place, pandemonium reigned. The troops marched back to the bus singing the Coast Guard song as loudly as they could; then they lifted Mr. Ischaar, Cris, Ramona, and Dallas up on their shoulders and marched two blocks down the street and back again singing *Semper Paratus* all the way.

During Saturday's final parade, The Torchlight, the band performed fantastically. Along the two-mile route there was never a glitch in the marching or the music, and the dedication to duty was mostly for Dallas because it was his very last parade.

At Seafair that year, the Coast Guard made a clean sweep: First place trophies for every unit in every parade. Such joy in victory! Euphoria danced around us all the way back to California!

Our years in the Coast Guard had been deeply rewarding. Though we had not gained much in monetary wealth, we were rich in fun, and faith, and friendship. And the lowly recruit band from Base Alameda had become the pride of the Coast Guard.

Friends and the Mouse

Our breezy little apartment in Oakland had one good point. Friends lived down the hall. Bryce and Anna-Marie were also in Oakland as a result of induction into the Coast Guard. They were new members of the Church, and the four of us were somewhat inseparable. We were especially glad to have each other when one of the men was on overnight duty at the base because the remaining husband could be the guard at home for both of us.

One night when Bryce was on duty and just as Dallas and I began to doze off to sleep, there came a "rap, rap, rap" on our door. Cautiously, Dallas went to the door and queried: "Who is it?"

"Anna-Marie," came the whispered answer. He opened the door to find our neighbor dressed in a billowy robe and puffy fuzzy slippers, pink curlers in her hair. "I'm sorry," she apologized, "but there's a mouse in my room." She giggled, in a panicky sort of way.

Dallas retrieved his robe and slippers and padded down the hall with her.

Afterwards he told me (and anyone else who might be interested, especially if Anna-Marie was in the vicinity) that this is what happened thereafter:

The two of them entered the apartment and peered about with uncommon stealth and cunning. With the bed down from the wall in the living room, there was barely room to walk around it. Suddenly there was a scritchy-scratchy sound in the corner, and a rodent approximately the size of Dallas's little finger, tail and all, scurried into the closet. Anna-Marie screeched and jumped up on the bed. Dallas followed the creature into the closet and picked up a lethal tennis shoe, Anna-Marie all the while eehing, ahhhing, and ooohing. Watching carefully, he adeptly moved in on the cornered critter. WHAP! The tiny terror never knew what hit him. Dallas, with sanitary precision, lifted the mouse by the tail and carried it to the bathroom where it was flushed into a watery grave.

Anna-Marie peered in the doorway, looking somewhat green. "Ohhhh," she moaned. "I think I'm gonna be sick." Dallas placed an invisible trumpet to his lips and solemnly tooted the tune of taps over the toilet.

I never did learn whether Anna-Marie's stomach actually reacted unfavorably to the circumstances. Dallas returned to our room chuckling. He knew he had just found some more good material for his occasional comic routines.

Friends and the Cat

Whenever Dallas and I had socialized with a group of friends long enough to be comfortable with them, it became a standard practice, at some point, for Dallas to size up the crowd, analyze the individual personalities, find one very sympathetic female who would really listen, then wait for an opportune moment to tell the story of the cat.

"Did I ever tell you about my cat?" he always began. After a chorus of "nos," he became uncharacteristically serious.

"Well, when I was a teenager, we had this beautiful Siamese cat. She was the pride and joy of the family, although I kind of ignored her.

"One day my parents were leaving on a trip to visit family members in California. Mom fixed a huge roast for me to eat while they were away and put it in the refrigerator. They left very early in the morning so I got up and had breakfast a little later, before I left for school. I guess I didn't see the cat jump up into the refrigerator as I put the milk away.

"Later, when I came home after work, I opened the refrigerator to get some roast for dinner and there was the cat, cold and shivering.

"Well, I panicked. I took her from the refrigerator and laid her on the floor. She was gasping and shaking. I quickly looked up the phone number of a vet who lived in the ward and hastily explained the situation to him. He said I needed to use something to shock her system, to get her moving again. He asked if we had any alcohol in the house. I assured him that we did not. 'Any rubbing alcohol?' he countered. I didn't know of any.

"He thought for a minute. 'You go camping, don't you?' I verified that fact. 'Do you have some white gas, the kind used in camp stoves?' I was sure we did. He, then, gave me careful instructions: 'Get a little white gas. It must be white gas. Other gasoline has lead which is deadly. Get a teaspoon and pour just a little down the cat's throat.' I hung up and rushed to find the camp stove.

"In my haste, I didn't listen carefully. I grabbed a tablespoon instead of a teaspoon, filled it with gas, cradled the gasping cat in my arm and poured the liquid down her throat.

"Only a second passed. The cat screeched and sprang from my lap. She ran, pell-mell, across the kitchen, jumped onto the dining room table, back to the floor, tried to climb the curtains, leap-frogged to the living room and across the furniture, and then ran in circles around and around the living room rug. I stood by, unsure and afraid of what I should do. Finally the cat collapsed, motionless, in the center of the room."

After the story's dramatic crescendo, the mesmerized crowd was silent and so was Dallas. They waited for him. He waited for them. Always, the previously designated and by now profoundly sympathetic female would cautiously, quietly, ask the question which hung, gravely, in the air.

"Was...it...dead?"

"No," he answered, as a smile began to form around the corners of his mouth. "Just out of gas."

As the poor gullible girl realized she'd been hoodwinked, she would first gasp for breath, then attempt to hurl some insult in Dallas's direction before throwing the nearest pillow at him. She was just the scapegoat for the others who were simply more reluctant to ask the dreadful question. Dallas just guffawed and chuckled as he put his bag of tricks away until the next unsuspecting audience came along.

Even if someone in the group had seen the routine before, they never issued a warning to the rest. I was the only one who sometimes had to leave the room in order to not give the joke away too soon.

And, I don't know how he did it, but his skill at involving people in the story was so effective that, once in a great while, he could even catch the same unsuspecting girl twice.

A Music Lesson

During the time when Dallas directed the Coast Guard band, there was a captain in the district retiring from the military who had rubbed the bandmaster (and other local military personal) the wrong way at least a dozen times in the previous couple of years. When, with his usual lack of tact, he "commanded" the band to play his state song at the retirement ceremonies, it was the last straw.

"Honestly," Dallas said to me, "sometimes people can be so 'Mickey Mouse.'" That was military jargon for juvenile, ridiculous, foolish, intolerable, unnecessary, basically a pain in the neck.

For several days Dallas, a normally kind and cooperative guy, grumbled about having to do favors for such a disagreeable person. Then his creative talent took over. At the small keyboard in our small living room he labored for almost a week, long after midnight, writing a new counter melody for the trombone section and arranging the music for the requested song so that all parts blended well together. In the end, the sleepless nights were worth it.

I went with him to the last rehearsal in the band room. When we walked into the dismal gray military barracks, the band was already assembled and in their seats. As Dallas bellowed for quiet, I noticed that he was trying to fight back a silly grin.

"For the last two weeks," he began, "you've been practicing a special arrangement for the Captain's retirement. Now I want you to know that this is not a traditional version. What you hear now, I expect you to hold in complete confidence." His imprisoned smile found freedom. "I've never let you play the parts to this song individually until now. Trombones, play your part without the other instruments."

The trombones began to play but, after only a few measures, the entire band broke into hysterical howls of laughter and so did I. Dallas had done his job well. As a counter melody, the trombone section was playing the Mickey Mouse Song.

"And now that we all have a secret," Dallas said when the laughter subsided, "I hope we can all maintain our military composure." Fifty faces smiled at him in assurance that they would not fall apart.

Later on the drill field, as the band serenaded the Captain, the disagreeable leader listened in rapture to the familiar tune but the band members heard only the trombone section's enthusiastic rendition— and I was sure they all wanted to sing along: "Mickey Mouse, Mickey Mouse, forever let us hold our banners high (high, high, high)! Come along and sing this song and join the family: M-I-C-K-E-Y—M-O-U-S-E."

Even so, they maintained expressions of perfect serenity until the last glorious notes drifted into oblivion.

After the troops passed in review, Dallas dusted off his blue uniform and joined me.

"It was beautiful," I whispered.

"It sure was, wasn't it," he grinned.

We walked to the edge of the parade field together where Dallas bid the Captain a truly fond farewell. The Captain put a pudgy hand on Dallas's shoulder.

"Beautiful rendition of my state song, Archibald. Very beautiful indeed."

From what Dallas had told me I was sure that, despite all the statuettes in the trophy case, this was the first compliment the Captain had ever given him.

Dallas turned his smirk into a smile. "Thank you, sir," he responded eagerly. "I arranged it especially for you."

A Night in the Trunk

When Dallas and I were first married, we discovered that we had a difference of opinion about spending days, weeks, or months in the great outdoors. Had we been able to afford a motor home, Dallas could and would have converted me to outdoor life very quickly. However, wealthy we were not. Dallas tried unceasingly to push me out of our apartment and into a tent on weekends, but I was hardly a willing subject. To me, a vacation in the out-of-doors meant a week at Yellowstone Lodge. The idea of sleeping with the beasts, birds, and bugs was mentally terrifying. In fact I was certain that, under those conditions, I wouldn't sleep at all.

But then one day, quite unexpectedly, things began to change.

One evening Dallas staggered home after a long week of military "Mickey Mouse" stuff looking like he was in need of more than chilled root beer and tuna casserole.

"That bad?" I asked as he sank into the living room chair.

He just groaned.

As we talked it over, I mused, "I think you need a vacation."

He chuckled. "Right. A week in the Swiss Alps and I'll be as good as new."

I was silent for a few seconds thinking of how much the man I loved needed a rest. Then I heard myself quietly mumble, "Well, maybe we could go camping." I winced, even as I said it.

"What?" Dallas didn't quite understand me, or at least he thought he hadn't.

I cleared my throat. "Well, ahh, well, maybe we could go camping. You and me."

Dallas laughed. "Thanks," he said, "but I would spend the whole time worried about your relationship with the bugs."

I couldn't think of a rebuttal, and the subject died.

However, the very next evening when I got home from work he met me at the door, smiling widely. "Were you serious about going camping with me?" I swallowed hard and forced my head to move up and down.

"Then, I've got it all figured out," he said. "Come on. I'll show you."

"You've got what all figured out?" I asked.

"Come on," he repeated.

He directed me outside and to the back of the car.

"See how wide the car is?" Dallas asked as we approached the rear of our midnight blue 1959 Plymouth sedan. "It's six feet wide. If I take the spare tire out and fill in all the cracks and crevices so it's completely flat, I figure we can both sleep in there."

"We can both WHAT???!!!"

"Sleep. Look, I know you don't like camping out, but this really wouldn't be like camping out at all. The bugs and the animals couldn't get to you. You would be safe and sound, and we could afford a vacation. We have sufficient funds to pay for one night at a cute little inn I learned about; but we would need to spend one night somewhere else, cheap."

"But...but...that sounds dangerous. Climbing into the trunk and closing it?"

"No, it wouldn't be," he said with absolutely certainty. "The latch can be fixed so the trunk won't lock, and then we'll just tie down the trunk lid leaving a few inches of space for air."

"I don't know. It sounds kind of crazy."

"Well, we're a little crazy, aren't we?"

I knew that one of us was for sure. But just the thought of a trip to the mountains had changed Dallas's attitude and countenance so completely that I couldn't think of a way to counter his suggestion.

"I guess we are crazy," I agreed. "When do we leave?"

"There's a long duty-free weekend coming up. We can leave on Thursday night."

"Okay." I tried to sound enthusiastic. "Let's do it." I went off to fix dinner, but I found I wasn't really very hungry.

The weekend rolled around much too soon to suit me, but not so with Dallas. He spent his spare time tinkering with the car, borrowing sleeping bags and camping equipment, and remodeling the trunk. He eventually had the trunk transfer down to a science. He could remove the spare tire and have our beds made in two minutes flat. He even invented a most ingenious portable bathroom. There were times when I thought innovation should have been his middle name.

And so, with a cooler full of drinks, sandwich staples, and a sack of junk food, we departed as planned.

As we drove the first night, we nibbled on potato chips and egg salad sandwiches and talked about possibilities for the future. We wandered around some back roads and finally found a quiet spot by a river. He parked the car close to a large oak tree and proceeded to effect the trunk transfer. He made our sleeping bag beds, we crawled into the trunk and tied down the lid. Once inside, I had to admit that the improvised bedroom was considerably more comfortable than I had anticipated.

Nevertheless, I couldn't sleep.

I shook Dallas about 2 a.m.

"What's that?" I whispered.

"What's what?"

"That noise?"

He listened. "It's an owl," he moaned and went back to sleep.

I shook Dallas about 3 a.m.

"What's that?" I whispered.

"What's what?"

"That noise."

51

He listened. "It's just a deer walking down the river." He sighed and went back to sleep.

I shook Dallas about 4 a.m. He didn't respond and I couldn't bear to wake him again so I listened uneasily to the unfamiliar sounds outside and stared at the crack in the trunk. Finally I dozed off about 6 a.m.

A half-an-hour later Dallas woke up, untied the rope, and bounded out of the trunk. I forced one eye open. "Is it morning? Already?"

"Yup. Let's be off."

I groaned and crawled out.

We ate chocolate doughnuts on the way north and were settled at the country inn by 10 a.m. To my way of thinking, this was living. I curled up with a book and Dallas went fishing. Time passed too quickly. I slept well that night, and the next day we drove home.

One day a few weeks later, Dallas came home with the same grin on his face that I had seen so often before.

"I've got something to show you," he said taking a photograph from his pocket.

The picture was of a small white wooden trailer that appeared to be about 4 ½ feet high and 6 or 7 feet long. Then he handed me another picture which was of the same trailer, only this time instead of being only 4 ½ feet high, it was about 7 feet high. Comparing the pictures, I could see that the trailer had collapsible sides which folded down under an adjustable roof.

"Isn't it neat?" He was practically cheering.

I stared at him, not comprehending.

"A friend of one of the guys on the base made it. Now he's selling it and only wants $150 for it. The tires are worth that much."

"But...$150!"

"Don't panic," he said calmly. "I have a raise coming next month—and have arranged six months to pay." He threw his arms around me.

"Just think. We can get away from here once in a while and you'll be inside, safe and sound. It won't really be like camping out at all."

I was sure I had heard him say that before.

The camper was beautifully made and was just big enough for two with plenty of storage space under the beds.

After that, we often spent our free time beside a lake or river with the little white camper. It was our home away from home, even to me. When we left California, we took it with us and it followed us around for most of the next ten years.

Then, before leaving on an international assignment, we sold it to good friends for $1 and I dropped a tear or two. I knew it was worth so much, so very much, in memories. In its simple, rustic way, it was filled with candlelight and hearts and flowers.

TRANSITIONS

When we left California and the Coast Guard, our intentions were to return to Utah where Dallas would major in music at Ogden's Weber State College. We envisioned that we would eventually settle down in the Cache Valley mountains of northern Utah and there Dallas would teach junior high or high school band. We found a nifty little apartment in Ogden where we could spend the two college years, Dallas got a part-time job at a department store, and I landed a secretarial position in a real estate office. At church we were called to teach the young adults, who were almost the same age as we were, and we settled in for the duration.

Dallas's college schedule was filled with music classes and band and orchestra performances. The first semester provided very little free time. In spite of his intense timetable, he enrolled in a Spanish class because it was fun for him and helped him keep his language ability polished. When he registered for the second semester, however, the music department told him they would not approve his schedule unless he dropped the Spanish class.

Reluctantly, Dallas went to tell his Spanish professor who countered this news with a question: Did Dallas realize that he could graduate with a degree in Spanish in just two semesters? Dallas was more than a little surprised. He hadn't considered such a thing and had never checked into the possibilities.

We talked late into that night, and we prayed. The next morning Dallas walked into the registration office, dropped all his music classes and changed his major to Spanish. With that decision, we had no idea where the future might take us.

A month later, Dallas noticed a bulletin at Weber State announcing interviews with a representative of the American Institute for Foreign Trade (AIFT) in Glendale, Arizona (now TGSIM—Thunderbird Graduate School of International Management). Dallas signed up and, at the meetings, the interviewer and Dallas were favorably impressed with each other. Dallas was asked to apply for admission and he and I began discussing serious transitions again. Enrollment at AIFT would be expensive. It would probably set us on an international course with worldwide assignments. We prayed, we pondered. We read our patriarchal blessings over and over—all, it seemed, to no avail. We received no specific inspiration. Finally, we decided there was no over-riding reason for him to resist applying for admission to AIFT. So he did, and he was accepted. Because he had served in the military, he could use GI Bill loans and entitlements for the educational expenses.

Then, one day soon after, I found the confirmation we had been seeking. I do not know why we had not seen it during our quest for inspiration. I was reading Dallas's patriarchal blessing when the phrase leaped off the page at me: "I bless you at this time with the gift of discernment for this will be very necessary for you to exercise as you labor among your fellowmen in various parts of the world." Then I knew we had made the right choice and we were facing the right direction.

That August, Dallas graduated from Weber State with honors in Spanish literature; and a few days later, our car and camper loaded with much more than we would need that year, we were off to Arizona. After short visits to every national park along the route, we drove into campus and set up house in cozy but comfortable apartment #2 of the brand new married students' dorms. Our neighbors to the left were from Cuba, to the right from New York, and around the corner lived the other LDS couple on campus, Jeff and Barbara Marchant, as well as a couple interested in the Church, Steve and Karen Strawn.

Dallas studied full-time, except for a couple of weeks at Christmas when he worked on the switchboard in the office in order to earn a few extra dollars to buy a new suit for job interviews in the spring. I worked at a bank in Phoenix, thirty minutes away.

The atmosphere on campus was very informal and the camaraderie was unique, in part because of the multitude of students from dozens of countries around the world.

One day Dallas and a neighbor (an Irish-Mexican-American) were in our apartment drinking pop and playing chess in their lounging clothes, singing Spanish songs at the top of their lungs, when there came a knock on the door. *"Pasen ustedes!"* (Come in!) they called out with wild abandon. When the door opened, there stood the campus Vice President and a group of official Asian delegates wanting to look at our apartment. Dallas and his friend scrambled, trying to look dignified enough to guide the dignitaries through an official thirty-second tour of our crowded and rather cluttered accommodations.

We had dances, swim meets, barbeques, sporting events, and ordinary get-togethers at each other's apartments, sometimes for no reason at all, other times for birthdays or special occasions such as the day friends down the corridor became American citizens.

Second semester excitement revolved around interviews, and it was a very good year. Dallas interviewed seriously with some thirty companies: advertising companies, grain companies, banks, retail organizations. Originally he gravitated toward advertising, but he finally decided against the intense, time-consuming life style. We often discussed the options and possibilities, wondering what the future would bring.

Then, in mid-April, he flew home from an interview in the midwest to say he had tentatively accepted a job in sales and marketing with Hallmark Cards. The enticement was a short summer training program in Kansas City, then to Japan for three months to learn the international military market, followed by an assignment in the 7,100 islands of the Philippines. I set my usual caution aside and joined in his jubilation.

Suddenly the graduates had marched in, the speeches had been given, and the diplomas had been awarded. The crazy social life was over and all our friends were departing for distant destinations. Jeff and Barbara and Steve and Karen were going to Ohio. The former left at the first possible moment with their new baby boy. We delayed, and that evening stood by our car in the middle of a rather deserted campus visiting with Steve and Karen who asked us if we might come to Ohio later that summer. With no hesitation, Dallas suggested we certainly would arrange it if they wanted to be baptized. To our delight, they said that sounded like a good idea.

And so, at the end of that short summer in Kansas City, we made the trip to Ohio for a memorable reunion—and moments in white—with the Marchants and the Strawns. Then we headed west: a stop in Utah for last minute farewells, and an exotic weekend holiday in Hawaii enjoying sand and sea at company expense.

The sun was shining brightly and the trade winds softly blowing when, with gifts of pink and purple leis around our necks, we boarded the plane in Honolulu for the flight to Tokyo. Even as we flew, we couldn't believe that we were on our way.

WORLDWIDE
SNAPSHOTS

Since we would only be in Japan three months for training, we lived in a hotel in Yokohama. Getting around a new place can always be tricky, but that is especially true with an unfamiliar alphabet. Dallas, however, dove into the language and learned enough in a couple of weeks to get us where we needed to go. I just followed along—whether on foot, in taxis, or on trains.

We walked the hustle-bustle streets of Tokyo and other giant cities and took taxis to neatly trimmed ceremonial gardens carefully hidden away in quiet corners. We took the train to famous shrines: Kyoto, the elegant royal city in the south; and, to the north, the spectacular mountain retreat and national park at Nikko which was dressed for us in the vivid red and gold of autumn.

One Saturday we hopped into the tiny car of another Hallmark representative, Max Bissey, and the three of us headed off enthusiastically in search of the giant statue of Buddha at Kamakura. We were not deterred in the least by the indecipherable map we hoped to follow or by our minimal ability to communicate in Japanese. We navigated the twists and turns of the city with no difficulty, but once in the countryside we lost our bearings and the map covered with Japanese squiggles was no help whatsoever.

As a result, our methodology for continuing the journey consisted of Max pulling to the side of the road whenever we saw someone of local origin. Dallas would then lean out the window (or even step out and dip from the waist in a couple of Japanese bows) and ask with Spanish accented Japanese, "*Daibutsu, onegai shimasu?*" (Where is the Buddha, if you please?) The person of local origin would then spew forth several hundred Japanese words (or so it seemed) and point in the direction of the Buddha. Before we rushed on, Dallas would conclude with gratitude: "*Domo arigato*" (Thank you). Since we actually had no clue as to the substance of the commentary received, we would head off in the general direction of the pointing finger until we met the next person of local origin. Then the little drama would play itself out all over again.

Dallas had a wonderful time with this charade and when, finally, we rounded a corner into the parking lot at "*Daibutsu, onegai shimasu,*" we praised Dallas for his extensive linguistic ability which had brought us safely to our destination.

(Two years later on our way home from the Orient, we went back to visit Japan and Dallas refreshed his Japanese. A few months after that we visited Nogales, Mexico. We parked on the U.S. side and walked across the border to do some shopping. Midway through the day, we took a taxi to a restaurant. After paying fare and tip, we exited the taxi as Dallas, quite unconsciously, offered a thank you in his most recently used foreign language: "*Domo arigato,*" he acknowledged, graciously, to the duly perplexed Mexican driver.)

After three months in Japan, we were off to the 7,100 islands of the Philippines. In minutes we were captivated by the sunny skies and smiling people. English was the language of note, the Philippines having been an American territory for many years until independence was granted in 1946, but Dallas also learned a few words of the local Tagalog dialect. He tried all the foreign foods, including one he had trouble swallowing: Balut—duck eggs close to hatching, a major source of nutritious calcium and nauseating sulfur fumes. He adopted the local costume: the Barong Tagalog—a loose, cool, embroidered shirt worn outside the trousers. We both worked with the youth at church and even attended a couple of youth conferences, complete with Filipino fun and food, at a lodge in the mountains.

Since we were just out of school, with bills still owing, and since we vowed to see the Orient before returning to U.S. soil, we conserved our funds by moving into a new but barely furnished apartment with no hot water (a tolerable situation in a jungle climate). The building was separated by a wall from a vacant field frequented by water buffalo that loved the mud holes.

The Philippines was a real togetherness time for us. We did paper-work together, church work together, shopping together, laundry together. Dallas spent much time on the road servicing Hallmark displays at both commercial enterprises and at the military bases which were busy centers of activity during that time of the Vietnam War. I often went with him in his travels, reading a lot of books and seeing a lot of sights along the way.

We traveled the islands north, south, east, and west passing by majestic active and inactive volcanoes, rippling rice paddies, shimmering waterfalls, lithe palm trees, and driving down ribbons of highway lined with colorful banks of wild tropical flowers.

We walked on the hallowed ground of World War II history: the island of Corregidor where U.S. and Filipino soldiers valiantly but vainly defended the entrance to the harbor against the invading Japanese; the torturous path of the tragic Bataan Death March; and the elegant, reverent simplicity of the American Cemetery where thousands of U.S. soldiers are buried under an endless expanse of green grass and white crosses. We went to Mactan in the central islands where Ferdinand Magellan once stepped ashore; and we visited friends at a small Baptist hospital far to the south, several hours over a dirt road in a remote area of Mindanão. On any journey, Dallas always took along a fishing pole, just in case.

Our favorite place, our retreat in the Philippines, was Baguio City in the northern mountains. There it was crisp and cool and the lodge where we stayed was cozy. Baguio felt just a little like being back in the Rockies.

On one particular trip to Baguio when we had scheduled to stay some extra time, the announcement of an approaching typhoon convinced us to change our plans. If the storm produced road or bridge damage, we could be stuck in Baguio for days. That would have been nice personally, but responsibilities would not permit.

We packed in haste and Dallas finished his business as quickly as possible. Unfortunately, the rains had already begun as we headed down the mountain's hairpin turns. There was a river about halfway down the mountain where a bridge had been washed out in a previous storm. On the trip up to Baguio, the water was low and, going slowly, we crossed the river easily by simply forging it with our trusty blue sedan. Going down the mountain, however, would be different.

When we approached the river, we could see that the water was rising rapidly; but our only choices at that point were to attempt a crossing or to return to Baguio. We said a prayer, felt no impression to turn back, took a deep breath in unison, and inched into the water.

Slowly, very slowly, we crept forward. The water was swift and high. If we had rolled down the windows, we could have put our fingers in it. The river bottom was silt and gravel. We could feel the car slip on the uncertain surface. Floating down the mountain via the river and numerous waterfalls was not a pleasant possibility. Still, it was easier to go forward than backward at that point; and, though we were tense, we had no premonition of danger.

Seconds passed but seemed like minutes, or even hours. The crossing seemed to take forever as the river rose an inch or two higher. With just a few yards left, we felt a more sure traction beneath us and soon the car rolled up the bank onto reasonably dry ground. We breathed a collective sigh of relief and looked back to survey from whence we came. Only then did we realize that we had lived a miracle. The river was wider and higher than even we had realized when in the middle of it, and the water was swifter. We felt sure that we would not have made it across without Divine intervention.

Perhaps most miraculous of all, the car was still purring, waiting patiently to continue the journey.

Our time in the Philippines was peppered with many other instances of protection and direction; but perhaps the greatest miracle was that, when the assignment ended, our education loans were paid and there was enough money in the bank for that trip we planned. After fond farewells to a place and people we loved, we boarded a plane that took us to visit Singapore, Kuala Lumpur, Penang, Bangkok, Hong Kong, Taipei, and Tokyo. And the sacrifice to save the funds was well worth it. Every stop was full of museums, shopping, people, history, exotic food—and merited a roll or two of film.

We rented a motorcycle in Penang and Dallas motored around the island with me clinging on behind. In Bangkok, he ordered Thai curry for dinner thinking that he could handle any hot pepper in the world but learning, as his eyes began to water and smoke curled up from his ears, that Thai pepper has more kick than anything Mexico has to offer. In Hong Kong we almost broke the bank saving money on really good buys, and Dallas was in some kind of salesman's heaven haggling down the prices.

The three-week journey home was filled with smells and sights and sounds which would create indelible memories, haunt us with nostalgia as years went by, and teach me many valuable lessons.

Things A Baked Alaska Taught Me
    by Linda R. Archibald (© by Intellectual Reserve, Inc.; Previously published in the *Ensign* magazine; February 1979; 66-67; used by permission.)

Who would guess that a weakness for gourmet desserts would teach me persistence and determination?

It began as my husband and I traveled back to the United States after spending two years in the Philippines on a business assignment. For the entire twenty-four months, those "far away places with strange sounding names" had been calling us relentlessly. Therefore, we conscientiously stored our pesos month by month, and two days before we left Manila, we converted our cash to travelers checks and plane tickets for Singapore, Kuala Lumpur, Penang, Bangkok, Hong Kong, Taipei, and Tokyo.

On the first evening of our trip, after devouring a scrumptious feast in the Elizabethan Room of the Raffles Hotel in Singapore, we decided to indulge in a mouth-watering dessert—"Baked Alaska for Two." We requested it be served without the traditional finishing touch of flaming brandy.

A few minutes later, our smiling waiter presented us with a huge sphere of perfectly peaked meringue. He neatly sliced the pseudo-satellite down the middle and served half to each of us on elegant white china plates. Forks in hand, we quickly took the first bite and were enveloped in a delicious experience. The vanilla cake, less than two inches thick, was rich, moist, and slightly warm. The solid ball of pistachio ice cream was smooth and cold. The meringue was crisp, sweet, and hot. Before the tantalizing taste of the last morsel had vanished, we vowed to enjoy the euphoria of a Baked Alaska again soon.

Two days later, in Penang, we ordered our next white mountain. This one, a spice cake with vanilla ice cream, was served by a Moslem waiter who was delighted with our rejection of the brandy sauce and included a sermon on the evils of alcohol with his duties. The Baked Alaska we ordered in Hong Kong had a layer of fruit in it, and the one in Tokyo had rich chocolate nut ice cream.

Although the mysterious Orient is known for its many addictive influences, we may be the only travelers to have left there hooked on Baked Alaska.

After returning home and setting up residence in Albuquerque, New Mexico, my husband (being a creative cook) decided to concoct a Baked Alaska. In one of my cookbooks he located the recipe:

"Trim a layer of cake to desired size and top with ice cream. Make Meringue: beat five egg whites till soft peaks form. Add 2/3 cup of sugar beating to stiff peaks. Spread meringue over ice cream and cake sealing to edges of cake. Bake in 500 degree oven until golden—about three minutes."

"Nothing to it!" he concluded, slapping the book closed.

I wrinkled my nose. To me there was something terrifying about putting ice cream into a 500 degree oven.

It wasn't long before he realized that creating a Baked Alaska was not going to be as easy as it first seemed.

The cake was no problem. To make it less than two-inches thick only required baking it in a pan larger than the directions suggested. Then we sliced ice cream into squares, covered the top of the cake and, like brick masons, filled in the crevices when necessary. We tried all flavors of cake and ice cream: chocolate with vanilla, vanilla with chocolate, spice with vanilla, pound cake with black walnut, chocolate with chocolate, and peppermint with anything.

The difficulty was the meringue. Since whipping up a stiff meringue was not one of my talents, I was no help whatever. The meringue had to act like Styrofoam, totally insulating the ice cream against the 500 degree heat of the oven. On his first couple of attempts, the fluffy white mixture slid down the sides of the cake-and-ice-cream mountain like an avalanche, coming to rest on the cookie sheet below.

"If at first you don't succeed, try, try again," he sighed.

I'll never forget the night we had company and he decided to try, try again. As he finished beating the egg whites he lifted the electric mixer from the bowl without turning off the motor. White blobs splattered across the ceiling, windows, and faces of our guests. We mopped up, shoved the mountain in the oven, and through the window in the door watched the ice cream trickle onto the pan.

"Every great accomplishment was once an impossible task," he muttered, quoting some ancient philosopher.

In those days we ate a lot of cake and melted ice cream. But then, one glorious day, it happened. The meringue clung to the mountain, and when it came out of the oven the cake was warm, the ice cream was solid, and the meringue was crisp and hot. We took the first beautiful bite and were back in the Raffles Hotel.

The taste of success! How sweet it is!

Since then he's made Baked Alaskas by the score and not one has failed. He won because he refused to give up. Compared to other challenges he's faced, the Baked Alaska was a small one, but to him it was no less important. Only after the adventure of the Baked Alaska did I really understand the message of the plaque hanging on his office wall:

"Nothing in the world can take the place of persistence.

"Talent will not. Nothing is more common than unsuccessful men with talent.

"Genius will not. Unrewarded genius is almost a proverb.

"Education will not. The world is full of educated derelicts.

"Persistence and determination alone are omnipotent."

Traveling with Dallas was always an incredible journey. All I had to do was grab my passport and hold on. With him, more was always better. He was not afraid of the unknown and untried, not afraid to let his curiosity lead him into new places, unusual conversations. He became a trivia expert on a multitude of subjects because in taxis, in shops, on tours, or just with ordinary people, he asked a multitude of questions. Then, later, whenever a conversation touched on one of his areas of "expertise," he eagerly enchanted any listeners with his vast knowledge of fascinating details.

After our Oriental journey, we went to New Mexico on assignment with Hallmark for a few months. While there we visited countless nooks and crannies in that "Land of Enchantment" including the mammoth caves at Carlsbad Caverns and the rolling dunes at White Sands National Monument. During long talks during those long drives around New Mexico and a trip back to Arizona, we decided to return to AIFT (now TGSIM) where Dallas could, in one semester, finish his master's degree in International Management.

This time we lived off campus, a few minutes away in the town of Glendale, and I worked on campus in the alumni office. The semester whizzed by at the speed of light and once again Dallas was interviewing. He began by talking to banks and financial institutions thinking that they would be less likely than sales and marketing organizations to require extensive travel as part of the job, and he met with several before one wise banker pointed out the truth. He listened to Dallas's enthusiastic, convincing self-promotional pitch, then sat back in his chair and chuckled. "If you joined us," he chortled, "you would be bored in minutes." Dallas knew the truth when he heard it. He switched

67

to a sales and marketing focus and, after pondering and praying, decided on a career with NCH Corporation, a world leader in industrial chemicals based in Irving, Texas, a suburb of Dallas (which would thereafter make names confusing).

But our first location as members of the NCH team would be Grand Junction, Colorado on the western slope of the Rocky Mountains where Dallas would learn the ins and outs of commissioned sales before assuming a position in management.

The road territory in Colorado was another "two for the road" experience. Up and down the western slope of the Rockies we went. Dallas again adopted the local costume: cowboy boots, cowboy hat, and western slacks, shirts and jackets. He spent long days knocking on both corporate doors and barn doors looking for just one more order of solvents, cleaners, or fertilizers. I went along much of the time content with pen and paper, a good book, and his company. But the territory was so extensive and business was so challenging that the travel expenses were destroying any attempts on our part to remain debt free. Dallas came up with a solution to the problem by suggesting we buy a small, used, gray Dodge camp wagon (since our little white camper was not equipped with cooking facilities or insulation). He convinced me that the payments on the Dodge would be considerably less than the costs of motel rooms and dining out.

And so, we made the purchase and in sun, snow, sleet, or rain, we drove the territory by day and, in the evening, camped beside beautiful lakes and rivers with some of the most spectacular mountain scenery in the world as background. For dinner we often cooked fish which Dallas caught upon our arrival.

With Christmastime approaching, our bank account was barely in the black. Dallas, wanting to give all his customers personal Christmas presents, suggested cookies. I choked on the idea, thinking in terms of quantity. Nevertheless, during December I spent my days baking hundreds of little round almond cookies and in the evenings Dallas helped me dip them in green and red powdered sugar frosting and roll them in color-coordinated coconut. He was so enthusiastic about the down-home gifts that he couldn't have been any more excited if he had been passing out hundred-dollar bills.

That Christmas season was also moving time. We sold the Dodge camp wagon and, after a week of non-stop sorting, cleaning, and packing, we left in our small, over-loaded red Ford and white camper to spend Christmas weekend in Utah followed by a long, sometimes snowy, drive south to Phoenix and east to Dallas.

At Texas corporate headquarters, Dallas began a year of management training traveling as a sales trainer to New Mexico, Colorado, Kansas, Oklahoma, Louisiana, and Tennessee. Though the schedule was strenuous he, of course, enjoyed the work and often overwhelmed his trainees with enthusiasm.

"Can you get three orders a day?" I would hear him challenge them boisterously over the phone. Hesitantly, they would reply, "I'll try," which would prompt him to exclaim with fervor, "I don't want you to try. I want you to do it!" Once he had their attention, he would feed them oodles of encouragement.

After one year of training in Texas, we were off to Canada where Dallas would direct an international sales training program. That December, once again, we were driving together: north to Toronto in a dark green Cadillac Sedan de Ville with which Dallas had fallen in love and purchased at a bargain basement price from an elderly couple who had only driven it to the grocery store and back during the five years they owned it. He was gleeful about the immaculate care and the miraculous price.

In Toronto, he was renowned among the sales force for his ability to carry a forty-pound bag of chemical samples in -40 degree weather at a faster pace than anyone else. He reveled in the call of the legendary

Canadian wilderness where we scouted out the hunting and fishing wonderland and sometimes camped out in a green and yellow umbrella tent. We visited a winter carnival of amazing ice sculptures and traveled through the history of the Eastern United States. In August we hosted friends and relatives during the Hill Cumorah Pageant, a couple of hours to the south near Palmyra, New York.

It was after one of those trips to Cumorah that we arrived home in the wee hours of the morning to find a message telling Dallas to catch the 7 a.m. plane for Texas to attend an important corporate meeting. Later that day he called me with startling news. We were to leave Toronto immediately, return to Texas for four months, then move to Johannesburg, South Africa to open a new corporate office.

We had less than two weeks to pack and leave Toronto; and miraculously, we did it—mostly because, while I stewed and fretted over the impossible nature of the process, Dallas made decisions, created innovations, separated essentials and non-essentials, and forced miracles to happen. He knew I would always take care of the molehills once he had moved the mountains.

During our few months in Texas waiting for visas and paperwork to be completed, Dallas commuted on troubleshooting errands to Puerto Rico. One weekend I joined him for some memorable Caribbean romance. I packed my bag with new clothes and old jewelry and flew to the Latin version of my dream of a romantic evening at The Cliff House. When Dallas met me at the airport, my heart skipped a beat. We walked hand in hand on the beach, rented a car and drove around the entire island, took in a dinner show enjoying scrumptious food and the musical talents of singer Robert Goulet, and supped on other days at romantic out of the way places Dallas had discovered during his many alone hours there.

He loved being my guide, introducing me to every new experience with enthusiasm. Although, over the years, we spent a lot of time together, we didn't often take time to simply adore each other and enjoy being together. This Puerto Rican weekend was like the honeymoon we never really had. Though it wasn't our anniversary or Valentine's Day, I flew home deliriously happy and in love.

As we began preparing for departure to South Africa, Dallas suggested we take the long route—through South America. When we entered the world of international business, he had assumed he would be deluged with Spanish opportunities. Instead, we went first to the Orient and to Canada, and now we were preparing to leave for Johannesburg. He was beginning to think that the only way he would ever get back to South America was on a vacation; so we took that holiday by going to Johannesburg via Lima, Montevideo, and Rio de Janeiro.

Though we enjoyed Lima and Rio, they were just stopovers. The real purpose of the extracurricular travel was to return to Uruguay. During the few days we were there, Dallas introduced me to countless locations where, as a missionary, he worked, ate, and lived. He found people he had known and reminisced with them. We drove from Montevideo to the small towns of Colonia and Colonia Suisa where he had been a branch president, walked the quiet streets, and searched out more faces from his past. He had such a good time, he was almost giddy.

During those days, I began to understand his nostalgic Uruguayan memories. In Uruguay he had learned to be and become, to prioritize, to let go of things that don't matter and hold on tight to things that do. Wherever we went throughout the country, he was confronted by the euphoric feelings of such an education. Uruguay was a Never-Never Land of sorts to him, not because it was a playground, but because it was a place to learn about living and loving and lengthening your stride—a place where dreams begin to come true. Uruguay was a part of him, a lovely part of him, forever.

Once in South Africa, we learned to drive on the "wrong" side of the road—and Dallas was very tolerant about the dents and scratches on the car doors which resulted from my close encounters with various poles as I couldn't seem to get the right distance perception from the "wrong" side of the car.

Setting up a new office was time consuming, but church work and outings with friends filled any free time—and Dallas always arranged to have some free time. He was convinced that all work and no play would make Dallas a very dull boy.

We zipped around the Transvaal, the high plateau of central South Africa which is dominated by cosmopolitan Johannesburg and its gold mines, visiting historical sites and African cultural enclaves, and even curling up in sleeping bags for overnight stays at isolated fishing lodges. And when, much sooner than anticipated, Dallas's work in South Africa was deemed complete, we decided to combine our journey back to Texas with another sightseeing adventure.

We flew to the wild animal reserve at Wanke in Zimbabwe (then Rhodesia), and with cameras scouted zebras, giraffes, crocodiles, and lions—though the elephants eluded us. If Dallas had been on his own, he probably would have been out riding through the wilds in a jeep, traversing the bush with a sickle in hand; but, since I was along for the ride, he was kind enough to cater to my wishes and keep the adventure civilized.

From there we journeyed to tumultuous Victoria Falls. Because of the deafening noise of the falls and the cloud of mist sent up from the gorge by the roaring, cascading water, the natives long ago named it "the smoke that thunders." As we walked through the rain forest overlooking the falls, the constant spray left us dripping wet. The power and the beauty left us speechless.

A long flight took us to Tel Aviv for two days, just enough time to rent a car and visit the sacred history of Jerusalem, Jericho, and the

Dead Sea. Then we scooted on for two days in Greece, just enough time to sense the majesty of Athens and the quaint life on the islands in the sparkling, turquoise Aegean Sea. Finally, two more days were just enough to stop in Spain and walk the streets of regal Madrid and historic Toledo.

And through it all I just held on tight for the wild ride, grateful for the opportunity to see the world in the company of such a remarkable companion and guide.

Back in Texas once again, we decided to try and settle down. We bought a small but cozy condominium—and a sailboat. Since Dallas, Texas is not renowned for mountain streams and trout fishing, my Dallas was always looking for fulfilling ways to spend his occasional free moments there. When we returned from Johannesburg, he took me boat hunting—sailboat hunting. Dallas always loved the quiet motion of sailing. He even wanted to sky dive, hang glide, and pilot a glider. He was drawn to the sense of floating whether in air or on sea.

On the boat hunt, I (always cautious) argued for a small boat. He (always aggressive) said we could manage to fit a bigger boat into the budget. He won. We bought a 21-foot Buccaneer which had room enough to cook and shower and sleep six, and we docked it on a lake fifteen minutes from home.

Dallas would fly in on Saturday mornings from distant locations, and by 1 p.m. we were at the lake. We ate there, we tinkered with the boat, we read, and we talked. We invited our friends to join us for picnics and evening voyages up and down the lake in the moonlight. The warm quiet nights, the camaraderie, the gentle breeze, the slosh of the boat and the lap of the waves all contributed to a feeling of hearts and flowers.

On return to Texas I decided, with Dallas's encouragement, that it was a good time for me to resume university studies. So, while he traveled on troubleshooting assignments to the Caribbean and Mexico, I labored over textbooks on speech and hearing disorders at the University of Texas at Dallas. Then, on weekends, we delighted in sharing our different experiences.

I worked with the youth at church, but Dallas's schedule was difficult and unpredictable. Therefore, he was a home teacher; and one of the families he visited was Herb and Jeannie Fulkrod. Herb had joined the Church a few years earlier but, as a result, his first wife divorced him. He remained true and faithful to the gospel, and one day met a nurse named Jeannie. A few weeks later, Jeannie joined the Church. She was baptized in the morning, and that afternoon they were married.

Several months passed and Jeannie, through her medical training, noticed a subtle physical change in Herb. She suggested that he get a checkup. He followed her advice, but no problem was detected. Jeannie was certain that something was not right and so pressured Herb into another test. Herb was then diagnosed with a rare illness and given six months to live.

Devastated at the news, Herb asked for special permission to be sealed to Jeannie before the mandatory year since her baptism was fulfilled, but he was told the work could be done later, by proxy. Then Herb called his home teachers, Dallas and Brother Richard Brannock. After explaining the circumstances to them, he asked for a blessing. "I feel I have to live a little longer. I have to be sealed to Jeannie while I am still here, and I have much genealogy to do."

Dallas and Brother Brannock made an appointment with Herb for Sunday afternoon and they arrived fasting. Brother Brannock anointed with oil and Dallas offered the prayer. In that prayer, he promised Herb that he would live until his mortal work was completed.

Shortly after that, we moved from Texas; but, on a four-day return visit to the Lone Star State during a vacation, we received word that Herb had died the day before our arrival. We were fortunate to be able to attend the funeral. We thought it was amazing that we were in town at that particular time. Even more amazing, almost ten years had passed since Dallas, as a home teacher, had given Herb that blessing.

This time in Texas we felt more like we were "home" than at any other time and any other place since our marriage. Therefore, thoughts of departure were difficult. I was chopping onions in the kitchen when Dallas told me we had been asked to move again, to Mexico City. I blamed the vegetables for my tears. Nevertheless, Mexico was definitely calling us and I knew that if I refused to go I would regret the lost opportunities. Adaptable Dallas, of course, was thrilled to finally be returning to Spanish speaking territory. He agreed, however, that we needed to delay the move long enough for me to finish my last semester of undergraduate work and receive my Bachelor of Science degree.

Along with my final exams and graduation, we rented our condo and, after one last sailing Saturday, put The Boat in dry dock. With the farewells of dear friends at church ringing in our ears, we began our drive south—over the border, down Mexico way.

Getting settled in Mexico was no small task as our residence visas encountered a nine-month delay. While our household effects sat waiting patiently at the border for clearance, we lived simply—with a hide-a-bed and a card table.

One Saturday morning, six months after arriving, Dallas awoke very early with a strong impression to check the Mexican entrance papers on our brown Ford Mustang. A quick analysis indicated that if the car was still in the country at midnight that day, it would belong to the Mexican government instead of to us.

Before dawn, Dallas was in the car and on his way north to Texas. He crossed the border in the nick of time while I stayed behind to take care of Sunday responsibilities.

The Mustang never returned to Mexico, but at least it was ours to sell later. In its place we acquired a black Dodge sedan in which to explore the area: Aztec ruins, museums, cathedrals, handicraft markets, and wonderful restaurants. The airport also became a well-known site as we often found ourselves there intercepting friends and family members who were arriving to visit from points north. Dallas discovered a retreat at Refugio del Salto, a lodge beside a beautiful waterfall and lake some three hours from Mexico City in Valle de Bravo. He kept trying to find a way to bring The Boat south, but we could never justify it.

At NCH Mexico, Dallas's salesmen were outgoing, high flying "Peter Pans." They worked hard and they played hard. At one sales convention, I found them literally dancing on the tables, stomping to memorable Mariachi melodies; and Dallas joined them enthusiastically. Afterwards, in their memory, I hung a picture on my wall of a striped jungle cat with a quizzical expression on its face. The caption read: "If the meek will inherit the earth, what's going to happen to all us tigers?" I was pretty certain that Dallas's current group of "tigers" would quickly devise some innovative, festive, and probably noisy options.

In more sedate moments Dallas was the bishop of the Lomas Ward, a unit of some 100 English-speaking members. Since there were many opportunities for leadership and few members in the ward, Dallas simply told the youth that he knew they could assume positions of great responsibility and summarily called them to serve anywhere there was a need from nursery leader to ward clerk. Because he believed in their abilities, they began to believe in themselves.

Dallas was humor and fun and entertainment. He was spirituality and sensitivity and stability. And, quite often, he was compassion and spontaneity.

The Gringo Samaritan

Like a wide black ribbon, the busy thoroughfare of Paseo de la Reforma winds from downtown Mexico City to the western mountains and, on its route, climbs the hills of the elegant suburb called Lomas.

It was a weeknight at six o'clock on Reforma in Lomas. Traffic was heavy. A motorcycle with two riders swerved back and forth across lanes. Finally reaching the front of the pack of cars, it began to accelerate. Suddenly a Ford LTD darted swiftly ahead of the pack. The driver seemed not to see the motorcycle until too late. A terrible crush of metal sent the crumpled motorcycle skidding toward the curb. Two mangled bodies hurtled through the air. The LTD picked up speed and faded into the distance.

Car after car passed the grizzly scene on the right side of the road as residents and servants from the imposing houses lining Reforma peered through their wrought iron gates attempting to determine the cause of the commotion. Passers-by gaped at the blood. Seconds passed. Then minutes.

A black Dodge sedan inched up Reforma. The two American men inside—one a resident of the city, the other a visitor—were wondering out loud as to the cause of the extreme traffic congestion. Then, as the truck in front of them moved away, the men saw the bodies, bloody but conscious, one struggling to reach the other. And they saw that no one was helping. The black Dodge whirled quickly around the corner and stopped. Its two occupants ran toward the injured.

"Don't move," the one who had been driving the Dodge said in Spanish to the man who vainly reached toward the girl lying in the gutter. The man's leg was shattered. It would not move with him. His face was streaked with blood. From the girl's ankle, a stream of blood was beginning to flow down the street.

"Hold your leg here," said the driver of the Dodge, again in Spanish, indicating the pressure point to stay the flow. Then he yelled to a nearby spectator, "Call for an ambulance."

Seconds passed. Then minutes. A third man appeared curbside.

"*Soy un médico* (I am a doctor)," he said. Then to the injured: "Is this the man who hit you?" indicating the driver of the Dodge.

The eyes in the blood-streaked face strained, then his head moved from side to side. He had seen the man exit from the Dodge. "No. The car was an LTD."

The doctor turned to the two Americans. "An ambulance is coming," he said.

Suddenly a few more people joined the helpers. The two Americans turned and quietly left. The boy and girl on the curb would live, perhaps with scars, but they would live. As the black Dodge pulled away from the curb, a siren wailed in the distance. The two men knew they had done little, but had done what they could, and had done something when everyone else was doing nothing.

This was not the first nor the last time that the driver of the Dodge would stop on a road in a foreign country to help. Decisive, spontaneous, Dallas always felt a responsibility to be there for those in need.

In at least two ways, the Mexico experience was pivotal. First, our family of two very suddenly became a contingent of three. One day, a year-and-a-half after our arrival, both Dallas and I received a strong impression that the time had come to increase our family size. We prayed, made some official contacts, and two weeks later we were parents. The speed of the events was both overwhelming and consoling. We were certain that this was meant to be.

Dallas and I had waited a long time for Teresa Dawn (Teri), but she was worth it. We loved her from the first moment we saw her, and she and Dallas seemed to immediately develop a special bond. I think they must have sensed, early on, that they were blessed with compatible personalities. She was his little princess—adored, totally.

After two years in Mexico, the company assured us that we could stay there for quite some time and we had no complaints about that. One Thursday afternoon, rather spontaneously, we put a deposit on a condominium. That night in our prayers, we asked for confirmation of this decision—and that precipitated the second pivot point. The very next day our plans were abruptly and permanently changed.

CALLED TO SERVE

I had both hands in the washing machine that Friday when Dallas came in the door at lunchtime. Preoccupied with putting a load of clothes into the dryer, I didn't look up.

A few seconds passed before he spoke rather solemnly. "Can we sit down a minute. We need to talk."

Surprised at his demeanor, I dropped the soggy shirts back into the washer and checked to see that six-month-old Teresa was still asleep, wondering as I did so what event could require a formal sit-down conference in the living room. I could only think that something had gone wrong with the planned condominium purchase. I was in no way prepared for what he said.

"I just received a telephone call from President Romney."

President Marion G. Romney of the First Presidency of the Church??!!

My hands flew to my mouth as I gasped on an involuntary intake of air. Because we knew others who had received similar phone calls, his nine words instantly told me that he had been called to be a mission president. Without asking, I knew he had accepted.

I felt a lump crawl into my throat and didn't know whether it resulted from the humble honor of being called to such a position or from the realization that the call would necessitate a farewell to special friends, a special country, a life we loved, and a considerable amount of yearly income. It is possible, I guess, that the only element necessary to initiate the combination of fear, excitement, and humility which I suddenly felt was surprise, for the communication from President Romney certainly was that. The call to be a mission president came without any warning whatsoever. We had no idea that our names were even under consideration.

Lunch lasted longer than usual that day and we talked more than we ate.

President Romney's phone call came to the office at an inopportune moment. Dallas was the marketing director for the Mexican and Caribbean divisions of NCH. His regional managers were all in the office that Friday, involved in a friendly "tiger-style" debate regarding certain policies and techniques. Twice during the morning, the home office in Texas called. When Dallas's secretary rang to say the United States was again asking for him, he answered the phone in a tone of voice which did not mask his annoyance at another interruption. The voice on the other end remained completely composed, verified that she was speaking with Dallas Archibald, then calmly announced, "This is Salt Lake City calling. One moment please, I'll connect you with President Romney."

Dallas tried not to betray the shock he felt, but he must have failed for the managers were on their way out of the room before he began motioning for their departure. Feeling short of breath, he guessed immediately (just as I did later) why President Romney was calling; and during the ten-second eternity of waiting for the connection to be completed, he felt the same emotions as I did and foresaw the same farewells.

Finally President Romney came on the line joyfully asking, "Brother Archibald, are you related to the Archibalds in Idaho?" and they pursued a short discussion of family histories until President Romney changed the subject.

"Well, as you can guess, Brother Archibald, I didn't call to discuss your genealogy. I've been with the brethren this morning and we are now issuing you a call to preside over a mission of the Church. Do you accept this call?"

Dallas's acceptance was followed by several questions about health and finances. Dallas verified that his health was good, and considered adding: "Since I haven't had a heart attack in the last few minutes, I'll be okay for many years to come!" We were happy to learn such things as the fact that we would be given a living allowance and would not have to deplete our personal savings to accept the call; and that swimming, fishing and other low risk sports are not off limits for mission presidents and their families.

Dallas was not given our mission location which would be announced later, though we supposed that we would be assigned somewhere in South America; but July 1, 1979 was the date we would assume responsibility.

With lunch over and all the details of the phone call relived half-a-dozen times, we came face to face with the future. We had five-and-a-half months to prepare our temporal affairs so that we could leave them behind for three years. First on the list: cancel the condominium purchase in Mexico. That was accomplished quickly on Friday afternoon—with a forfeiture of part of the deposit money.

The weekend brought visits to friends and church meetings on Sunday. We had been told to keep the call confidential until we had the official letter in hand, but keeping the surprise a secret from everyone wasn't easy. The Lomas Ward was more like a big family than a congregation because all of us were away from our home country and we leaned on each other and connected with each other in special and unusual ways. As one week passed, then two, without the arrival of the official letter, the news became more and more difficult to keep.

Before President Romney's call, we had planned a vacation in Utah for the last week in February. After the phone call, it became imperative that we make that trip to the United States to begin the process of coordinating certain personal affairs. But, by the last week in January, it was obvious that revised business schedules would make an end of February trip impossible. If we were going to Utah at all we would have to leave on February 3 and return on February 10. We quickly notified family and friends, bought plane tickets, and departed on schedule Saturday morning—but without the official letter. We were beginning to wonder if the phone call had been real, something we planned to verify in Salt Lake City on Monday morning.

First, however, assuming it had been real, we stopped in Texas to set a few things in motion. By phone we had arranged for a real estate agent to meet us at the Dallas/Forth Worth Airport and, during our lay-over between planes, we listed our condominium in Irving for sale. Our renter had notified us the week before that she planned to move out in March, which seemed like a convenient coincidence. But, as we would soon discover, Someone Else was orchestrating the coordination of our temporal affairs.

While at the airport we also called an acquaintance who, for many months, had considered buying our dry-docked sailboat. We were so emotionally attached to The Boat that even though, after our move to Mexico, we had only used it briefly during a couple of trips to Texas, we had been reluctant to sell. Now the reluctance was gone. We gave the prospective buyer a final sale price and a two-week deadline to take it or leave it. Then, if he decided not to buy, we would offer someone a commission to sell it for us.

The remaining hour at the airport was spent in the restaurant eating ice cream with friends. When one of them jokingly asked if our sudden trip to Utah was the result of a call from the general authorities, Dallas and I instantly passed a silent question between us. Was the phone call a joke? Could these crazy Texans be the originators? I stuffed a spoonful of ice cream in my mouth and Dallas laughed artificially. No matter where we were, the secret begged to be set free.

Once in Utah, we advised a real estate agent that a piece of mountain property we owned which had been listed for sale for over two years needed to be sold immediately. Saturday night and all day Sunday we were with family and friends in Utah who asked endless questions.

"How long do you expect to be in Mexico?"

"When will you be home again?"

"Can we come to visit you this summer?"

We hummed and hawed and hedged until Monday morning finally arrived and, over the phone, President Romney's office verified that the call to serve had, indeed, been a reality. A couple of hours later we turned the secret into news after picking up a photocopy of the official letter, the original of which was apparently going by donkey train to Mexico. It would not arrive until February 15, five days after we returned from our trip.

On the Thursday before leaving Utah, our Texas real estate agent called to say that she had a firm offer on our townhouse at the best possible rates.

Our Utah real estate agent called the Monday after we arrived back in Mexico to say he had a firm offer on our long-listed mountain property.

The next day, Tuesday, the Texas boat enthusiast called to say he would buy our 21-footer.

One. Two. Three. Our business affairs were pretty well wrapped up, and it was only the middle of February.

But the biggest miracle happened on Wednesday.

Since the day of the phone call, we had been debating about how and when to tell NCH. Once we eliminated the secrecy of the call by having letter in hand, we realized we had to tell them immediately. They were proposing expansions into Central America and other changes in the area. To have delayed telling them would have been unfair.

Dallas called the office in Texas on Monday, February 12, saying he needed to talk to them as soon as possible. An appointment was made for Wednesday, giving them two days to imagine all sorts of haunting reasons for his sudden trip.

The company was headed by truly great men. They had always been caring and compassionate, "people oriented" was the company term. Still, Dallas left apprehensively. How would they react to the news that one of their upper-echelon managers was going off for three years on a church assignment? We envisioned everything from immediate dismissal to reluctant acceptance of the request for a leave of absence.

A vice-president and personal friend, Keith Asher, met Dallas at the airport and the two of them went to a spaghetti lunch talking about normal business matters. The spaghetti was half-eaten before the conversation lagged and Keith asked Dallas about the reasons for the trip.

"The Church has asked me to serve as president of one of the missions for the next three years. I need to ask for a leave of absence."

"That's exciting!" Keith responded enthusiastically. Then he dropped his fork in his spaghetti. "Did you say three years?"

There was a silent moment analyzing the true length of three years and the implications on current and future business. Then Keith relaxed and asked for details.

That morning, before Dallas's arrival, Keith alerted the other officers including the chairman of the board that an emergency meeting might be necessary. When Keith and Dallas entered the office after lunch, all were on hand and a high-level conference was convened.

It was this group that would make the final decision about our future once they knew the details.

Keith motioned to Dallas. "Tell them what you just told me," he said, yielding the floor. And so Dallas did. To his absolute amazement the Chairman of the Board, Lester Levy, immediately came around the table and gave Dallas a warm, loving handshake and hug.

"This is wonderful, Dallas. Though I don't understand exactly what you will be doing, I feel a sense of excitement. Don't worry," he continued, "we'll have an executive position waiting for you on your return and, while you're away, we'll keep all your benefits in force."

When Dallas called me from the airport in Texas to tell me the news, we both felt overwhelming gratitude for such special people and for the continuing miracles.

After that, life progressed on schedule and uneventfully until the first of April. General Conference had just ended and mission presidents' assignments had been concluded. This time we decided not to wait for "the donkey express."

Early Monday morning we called the missionary department in Salt Lake City and asked if we could be told the location of our assignment over the phone. A masculine voice informed us that the letters for new mission presidents were on the mail desk, that several new mission presidents had picked up their letters during conference weekend, and to wait a second until he found ours. Once located and opened it took only a minute for him to give us the news. Dallas hung up the phone and we stood staring at each other in shock.

SPAIN! We had never even considered it as a possibility. SEVILLE, SPAIN! Where was Seville? We got out the maps, found Seville (Sevilla) in the southwest, not far from Portugal on the west, Gibraltar on the south, and legendary Granada to the east, in the Spanish region known as Andalucia.

SPAIN! We really couldn't believe it and decided we had better have the official notice in hand before we began spreading the news, just in case the voice on the phone had read us the wrong letter. We had been so sure of going to South America.

But this time the secret was not official and we did not guard it well. We whispered it to so many people that by the time the letter arrived confirming the words of the voice, there was no need to make a formal announcement.

We changed our tentative air route from Texas-Utah-Los Angeles-South America to Los Angeles-Utah-Texas-Spain, and began final preparations with the usual contradictory feelings that accompany departures. Yes, the future was very exciting and, yes, we had said farewells many times before at various locations in the United States and overseas. But neither repetition of the experience nor anticipation for the future can eliminate the emotion inherent in saying long term, perhaps even permanent, goodbyes.

The company people, the "tigers" in Mexico with whom we had developed very close friendships gave us a giant farewell fiesta, a buffet dinner with roving mariachis. Music, love, and tears flowed freely that night and, in the end, friendships were bound together to endure regardless of time or distance. As a gift from them, we received a huge silver platter engraved with all their names. In return, we passed out copies of *The Book of Mormon* and explained why we were leaving as well as a little about their royal heritage as descendants of the tribe of Joseph.

One of the salesmen, Jaime León, took the floor for a short, spontaneous, emotional speech. In that brief moment he made a comment I would hear over and over again as time went by. "Dallas asked a lot of us, but he was never a boss. He was a friend."

On our last Sunday at church, Dallas was released as bishop and we both spoke, or tried to, after the Primary children sang "I Hope they Call me on a Mission."

At the airport a few days later, there were friends to bid our family goodbye; and, as we tearfully surrendered our Mexican residence visas at the immigration desk, Dallas explained our obvious emotional state to the official in charge: *"Los que piensan que es fácil decir adiós nunca han tenido que decir adiós."* (Those who think it's easy to say goodbye have never had to say goodbye.)

We headed down the corridor to our plane reflecting on the joys we had found south of the border; but as the jet soared north, our tears abated and our conversation modulated from memories of Mexico to thoughts about Spain, missionaries, and miracles. We had seen a few "magic" moments during our preparations, but there would be so many more.

Car Trouble

We were off on a fast weekend to district meetings on the eastern side of the Spain Seville Mission. There wasn't time for car trouble, but we had it anyway. We had been at the service station on the lonely mountain road for almost two hours trying to find a way to get the car to start again. But no matter what we tried, with or without the help of professionals, it didn't work.

Finally prayer was the only remaining option. As we whispered "Amen" to our request for assistance, Dallas's eye caught sight of an empty pop bottle placed in a pocket on the driver's door. He felt he should take it and bang on the fuel line. Feeling a bit silly, he did. Then turning the key, the car started. After a quick "thank you" to the attendants and passers-by standing around, we drove away and decided to go on across the mission in spite of the twenty-four hours of driving required rather than return home.

Along the way, we left the car running when we could. When we couldn't, we used the pop bottle. Finally Sunday night, safe and sound and on time, we rolled back home. But as we approached the driveway, the car stopped and no amount of pop bottle pounding would bring it back to life.

Monday morning it was towed to the repair shop.

Mission Success

Dallas spent endless hours conducting personal interviews with the missionaries. When there was a need to spend extra time, one-on-one, those conversations often lasted late into the night or even into the wee hours of the morning. He loved the elders and sisters, and with tender loving care he helped them find success and spirituality.

—He was one of those elders who came to the mission self-conscious and unsure of himself. But with carefully contemplated assignments and encouraging interviews from the president he began to change until, one day, he was called to be a new branch president in a distant city. Before his departure, I talked to him.

"I remember when you arrived," I said. "I remember how you felt compared to the others in your group." I felt a lump crawl into my throat. "Things have changed, haven't they."

He nodded. "Things have changed." His voice cracked and he blinked an extra time or two. "They've changed a lot."

He was confident, poised, charismatic, but humble. He was a miracle.

"He that is weak among you hereafter shall be made strong."
(D&C 50:16.)

—He decided to serve a mission to see if he could find a testimony. His unwritten position was that he would do all the right missionary things to see if a testimony would bloom. But his mission was nearing its end and, in spite of long conversations with the president and hard work, he hadn't found the treasure.

One night as we were passing through the city where he and his companion were to have had a baptism, we decided to stop by the chapel to see if the baptism had taken place. Entering the door, we knew it had for this elder was leaning contentedly against the wall by the baptismal font, smiling. He seemed surrounded by a halo of light, and we knew his search was over.

"Ask, and it shall be given you; seek, and ye shall find..."
(Matthew 7:7.)

—He should have been called to be a zone leader on this transfer day. That was the logical assignment for him. But Dallas, in prayer, felt certain that the Lord wanted him to be a district leader in one of the cities on the eastern side of the mission. And so the call to go east was issued, conversations ensued, and the elder humbly accepted.

And in that city he was like a magnet. People followed him. People came to hear him teach, groups at a time. People were converted. People were baptized. Lives were changed, including his.

"I'll go where you want me to go, dear Lord...." *(Hymns* 270.)

—Because of extenuating circumstances, he had been assigned to the mission office for a whole year and during that time he had been a junior companion. Finally, when the time was right for him to leave, he was given an assignment as a junior zone leader. His mission had just a few months remaining and the thought of spending all of it as a junior companion was more than he could bear. Still, it was two or three months before he wrote.

"Please President, send me into the field as a regular missionary. I don't care about being a zone leader. I only want to be a senior companion."

And so we drove out to see him. He explained and pleaded for the chance to be a senior companion, even if only for a few weeks. But the President felt strongly that he was in the right place and would end his mission there as a junior companion.

"Elder," he said, "for some reason the Lord wants you to learn to be a counselor," and then he added some comments about his being one day called to counsel among the leadership of the Church. The elder began to cry, presumably great tears of anguish, and the President tried to comfort him. But his response was, "No, President, you don't understand. You have just quoted from my patriarchal blessing. I will stay and be a junior companion."

"I'll be what you want me to be..." (Hymns 270.)

Dallas taught that God works in mysterious ways and, so, they needed only to believe.

—The senior companion awoke with a start, the dream still fresh on his mind; and he woke his junior companion even though the hour was early, too early to go tracting. "There is someone we have to find today" he confided, anxiously. "I have seen the hallway and the door to the apartment in a dream."

The two of them dressed, studied, ate and then strode urgently down the street. The senior companion knew the approximate location of the building they were seeking. At each building in the area he would enter and, taking the stairs two at a time, search the corridors earnestly for the sought for apartment.

One building then two, three, four, and five were canvassed. Finally, on the top floor of the sixth building, he recognized the doorway and motioned for his companion to follow in haste.

They knocked. A woman dressed in black answered.

"Come in," she said without hesitation or introduction. "I've been expecting you."

Faith precedes the miracle.

A New Day

Because Dallas invited *A New Day* to stay at the mission home, I experienced a miracle. *A New Day* was a musical group from the LDS Institute of Religion at the University of Utah. They were coming to Sevilla the first of June as part of a tour of Spain and Italy. We had scheduled them for two Saturday evening performances and a Sunday fireside in Sevilla; but on Saturday morning, the day they were to arrive, they called from Madrid in despair. The buses from Germany in which they were to travel, sleep, and eat had been delayed. No one knew when they were expected.

With the Sevilla performances just hours away, emergency measures were planned. A small nucleus of the group, fifteen singers and dancers and one piano player, would catch the fast train to Sevilla at 1 p.m. The mission cars would meet the train and take them directly to the theater. After the second performance, the cars would bring them to the mission home, arriving about midnight.

As far as I was concerned, there was just one complication in the plans. Arriving and departing missionaries had been staying at the mission home throughout the week, the house was very dirty, and every towel and sheet needed to be washed. Additionally, the supply of food in the refrigerator and pantry had been radically depleted.

I began about noon, worked through until late afternoon, hurried to the store for food (6 meals for 16), and returned home to work at full speed again. Up and down the two flights of stairs in the mission home I ran juggling washing, ironing, cleaning, sheets, towels, and two-year-old Teresa. About 10:45 p.m. Teresa, who was always up late following Spanish tradition, finally reached her limit. Bored and tired, she screamed for attention. I was ready to collapse. With one short hour left and much still to do, I could see no way to have everything finished. Yet I felt an obligation to do so. I was sure the performers of *A New Day* had not slept much in two days and probably not eaten either. They deserved food and rest. Somehow I had to be ready at midnight. But how?

I felt tears of exhaustion sting my eyes as I picked up Teresa. We sat down on a kitchen chair and I bowed my head.

"Father, if I'm to have everything ready by midnight, I need thy help."

A feeling of peace calmed my frayed nerves, and the next thing I knew I was standing in the kitchen in clean clothes fixing sandwiches. Teresa was in bed asleep, the guest beds were all made, and the last load of towels was tumbling in the dryer. An hour had passed but the events of that hour were a blur. I couldn't remember then or later how the work had been finished.

When *A New Day* burst in, they were tired and hungry but enthusiastic.

"Were you at the performance?" they asked as they munched sandwiches and chips.

"No," I laughed and briefly outlined the events of my day.

"Oh, Sister Archibald," they exclaimed, "you must be more tired than we are. We'll sing for you."

And there in the kitchen at midnight, sandwiches in hand, they sang "I am a Child of God." Their rendition was more beautiful than any I had ever heard, but that's not the only reason my eyes filled with tears as I listened. At that moment I knew, as never before in my life, the truth of the words they sang for He had been there waiting with miracles to help me when I needed Him.

Later I told Dallas about the missing hour. He smiled and nodded knowingly. Apparently miracles were new to me but not to him.

A Man of La Mancha

As a Spanish literature major at Weber State, Dallas studied and loved the story of legendary Don Quixote—"The Man of La Mancha" as he was called in the theater production. I sat with Dallas as he watched the movie for the first time, at home on video. At the end of the film the book's author, Miguel de Cervantes, climbs a ramp from the dungeon where the story has unfolded, to face the council of the Spanish Inquisition. At that moment, Cervantes and Quixote become one: men with vision who refuse to be defeated—and inspiring words and music about dreaming impossible dreams soars.

As the scene faded from our TV screen, Dallas stood up, tears streaming down his cheeks: "YES!" he declared emphatically. "I *love* all that idealism!"

La Mancha, the home of Don Quixote, was within the boundaries of the Spain Seville Mission.

Europe, as a whole, was a difficult mission field; and Spain was part of Europe. Baptisms were hard to come by. Nevertheless, the Spain Seville Mission was doing quite well with some fifty baptisms per month, monumental by European standards but a pittance compared to the thousands coming into the fold in countries like Brazil and Chile. Dallas was a realist as well as an idealist. He accepted that Spain was in Europe not South America. At the same time, he knew the numbers could be higher while still baptizing true converts into the gospel.

Part of the answer, he believed, was to convince every missionary of the importance of the work they were doing. They needed to see themselves as a team with every member being an important component in bringing people to Christ.

With every group of new missionaries, Dallas demonstrated the power of the Atonement with an original visual aid. He filled a crystal goblet with bright yellow corn oil and, using it as a symbol of our mortal state, explained that each of us comes to earth pure and clean, full of light. However, as we move through mortality, we err and sin. Darkness enters because we become imperfect. To illustrate the darkness, he poured spoonfuls of grape juice into the goblet of oil. The juice sank to the bottom. He explained that the Fall created this situation and we cannot change it. We will sin and we will make mistakes and they contaminate the light. Additionally, he emphasized, we have no power or ability to remove the darkness. Without intervention, the "grape juice" will remain in the "oil" forever. Dallas would then pour more oil into the goblet illustrating that even though we can add more light to our lives through obedience and good works, the darkness will remain.

The only way to remove the darkness is for someone else to help. In the case of our errors and sins, when we repent, the Savior intervenes. Only He has the power to remove the darkness, the stains, from our lives. Dallas then produced a straw, inserted it into the oil and carefully sucked out all the darkness from the bottom; and he concluded, "Every day of our lives, we do things that add drops of darkness to our light. We must constantly rely on repentance and the Atonement of Jesus Christ to remove the darkness and make us clean, pure, and full of light again."

The core of their mission, he told them, was to help the people of Spain understand the reality and power of the Atonement and how it works to bless individual lives. They all needed to work together to bring souls to Christ.

About a year into our three-year assignment, Dallas decided to tackle the problem of a lack of teamwork. Brigham Young University was doing well in football that year and everyone was at least aware of the newsworthy nature of BYU's success; so, for the American missionaries, football was an appropriate medium for teaching a principle. But we also had a few Spanish missionaries and he didn't want to leave them out of the fun. He prepared an instructive and entertaining demonstration for zone conferences, hoping to encourage all the missionaries to effectively work together. He wandered the room pretending to be the matador, the quarterback, the linesman, and even the bull in the story which was punctuated with his characteristic sound effects as well as the occasional laughter and applause of the audience. I call his speech "The Long, Long Pass"—translated here from the original Spanish.

"There is, in Spain, something that Spaniards call art. I don't know that I'm in agreement, but they say it is art. This art form is the bullfight. It usually involves a man who is extremely thin and who wears a suit so tight that he can hardly walk. He carries a cape and a sword. And the art, they say, is the battle between the beast—the muscles and movement of the beast—and this thin *torero*.

"Well, excuse me Elder Brosa (or any other Spanish elder in attendance), but I want to talk about a North American art. I want to talk about the beasts of the field against other beasts of the field, and about another thin man—a man called a quarterback. Now in this art, we have this poor quarterback behind a line of "beasts" who are supposed to protect him, and one of these big "beasts" throws him an oblong-shaped ball. On the other side of the field there are eleven more beasts who weigh more or less 400 pounds each, ready for the battle. They are growling and snarly, ready for the fight with mouths open, smoke rising. And this poor quarterback is there, trying to stay alive.

"North American football really becomes an art when the team is just a little behind and it's almost the end of the game. The fans are on their feet screaming, and the players sense the spirit of the battle. They realize time is running out. The quarterback, this great quarterback, realizes he has to do something amazing. He has to move. He has to 'scramble.' He receives the ball. He begins to run, to run in circles, trying with all his might to do something magic while still remaining protected by his big beasts from the other big beasts who want to grind him into the ground.

"Let's say it's the last few seconds of the game and he has the ball. He begins to run, to move, to avoid the beasts. Then he sees one of his best receivers way down the field, free and in the open! He drops back, and he throws the ball! It's going, going, going! The receiver is watching it! It's coming closer! It's on target!

"———Now, let's stop the game here. ————What if the receiver at the end of the field suddenly thinks, 'Hey I don't want to do this. I don't want to be a receiver. I want to be the quarterback. I want all that glory. I'm not going to catch the ball.'

"Or, what if one of the big beasts who has to protect the quarterback suddenly says, 'Hey, I really want to be a receiver. I don't want to be a protector,' and he steps back and waves the enemy through.

"Now, let's speak of our own team; the missionaries of the Spain Seville Mission. All the positions on this team are very important. Some have to protect the quarterback, some need to be receivers, others provide support in different ways. Everyone has a calling on this team. And if someone on the line is jealous of the quarterback and, therefore, refuses to do his own job saying, 'go on through because I'm not important,' the team will lose. Everyone has to do their part.

"But the team we are talking about is a team where everyone does his part. And the ball is coming, flying! The receiver is waiting, watching, running—and the ball comes, landing perfectly in his arms! He crosses the goal line as time runs out—and the team wins the game!

"This, Elder Brosa, THIS IS ART!"

(Pause for laughter).

"I have presented this little drama for a reason. All of you know what can happen when a team really wants to win. Usually they do win, even when there are obstacles that make it difficult. They win because they work together to make it happen. We must all work together, be a team, to make many good things happen."

Two months later, the Spain Seville Mission totals rose to 85 baptisms in one month and everyone rejoiced because they knew they had done it by pulling together, helping each other. They had done it, united, with teamwork.

In the mid-1980s, just a few years after returning from Spain, Dallas attended an all-Spain missionary reunion. The announcer who was introducing the mission presidents in attendance at the cultural hall gathering managed to forget Dallas's name. During the moment of silence as he tried to remember, Dallas spoke just loud enough for everyone to hear: "They may forget the name, but they will never forget the statistics!" All the missionaries from the Seville mission rose to their feet, cheering.

To Dallas, nothing was ever impossible. He dreamed impossible dreams. Then he made the dreams come true.

BRAZILIAN HEART, BRAZILIAN ROOTS

When the door to Spain closed, the door to Brazil opened wide and stayed open for a very long time.

Brazil, beautiful land of the sun
Beautiful palm trees against a sky of blue
White beaches in the moonlight
Soft breezes from the sea.

The beauty of Brazil, by any standard, is spectacular; and Brazilians, by any standard, are among the most optimistic people in the world. Like bobbing corks with smiling faces, they effortlessly bounce back from discouragement and defeat. Dallas, obviously, fit right in. He understood them and they understood him. They all spoke Portuguese and they all spoke the language of hope.

When we went to Brazil following the mission in Spain, little did we realize that we would be there for almost fifteen years and during that time our roots would grow very deep. While Dallas and I called both the United States and Brazil "home," Teresa was growing up Brazilian. Once, as we were packing papers to take with us on a visit to Utah, Dallas and I were discussing the business we needed to transact when we got "home." Teresa, playing nearby, stopped to survey us curiously. "But, Daddy," she interrupted with some concern in her voice, "we are home!"

Yes. We were home!

It was in Brazil that I finally learned exactly where to find that elusive "second star to the right" so I could fly with Dallas "straight on 'til morning." (See *Sunshine in My Soul, Discovering the Magic in Everyday Life*; Deseret Book Co.; Salt Lake City, Utah; 1999.) And, in Brazil, Dallas taught the local population that "gringos" don't have to be foreigners.

As Dallas was a regional representative for the Church and was also trying to stabilize NCH in a country as large as the United States, he traveled much and had contact with many people. Because of his unpretentious nature and his unconditional love, people were drawn to him. Brazilian friendliness bubbled over when Dallas's contagious enthusiasm was in the area. Smiles blossomed on the faces of bellboys, desk clerks, venders on the streets, the NCH sales force, and church members and leaders as salutations rang out everywhere: "Oy, Elder Dallas!" "Oy, Senhor Dallas!" Equally comfortable with rich and poor, young and old, he went about trailing clouds of energy and inspiration; and sometimes I thought he was more Brazilian than the Brazilians themselves.

Once, while waiting for his flight in a Brazilian airport, he allowed a small boy-child to shine his shoes. After paying the agreed upon amount plus tip, he told the boy to go and round up his friends who were also proffering their polishing skills to travelers. When the half-a-dozen rag-tag children were gathered around him, he invited them to sit at his feet while he taught them—with his own shoes, handkerchief, and personal saliva—the techniques needed for effecting a radiant military spit-shine. Then he told them to practice the procedure because "spit is cheap, and a brilliant shine brings big tips."

Whether or not the "shoe shine boys" followed up on his advice is unknown; but, no doubt, they are still telling their story of sitting in a circle at the airport learning at the feet of a "gringo Samaritan."

Our home in São Paulo was in a wonderful apartment complex encircled by several acres of tropical beauty. We had many forever friends, and family time was special. We were fortunate to be able to spend holidays in spectacular places: the fabulous beaches of Rio, the grandeur of Iguaçu Falls, the splendid ruins at Machu Picchu, a nostalgic return to the history of Mexico City, and a delightful excursion to the sand and sea of Cancun. Once we visited friends in Europe; and, whenever possible, we established traditions at the Rocky Mountain get-aways of Wyoming's Yellowstone Park, Idaho's Sun Valley Resort, and Butterfly Lake in the high Uintah mountains of Utah. Everywhere we went, Dallas loved life and people loved him.

On one of our vacation summers, I had an opportunity to analyze his optimism in action.

Hard Breaks, etc.

We were vacationing in Sun Valley during the summer that Dallas reached the landmark age of fifty. He and Teresa were enjoying horseback riding, tennis, shopping, and ice skating that year. I was enjoying a long relationship with a number of good books. That Tuesday morning, husband and daughter had gone to the outdoor ice rink early for skating lessons. I lagged behind, finally taking book in hand and heading out on foot toward the bleachers by the rink. As my destination came into view, so did an ambulance with siren on heading in the same direction and something whispered to me that life was about to hit a bump.

I increased my pace a bit and rounded the corner to see Dallas, flat on his back on the ice, paramedics approaching, and Teresa standing silently nearby. Their teacher, Lorna, skated toward me.

"What...?" I began, but she interrupted.

"He says he has a broken leg. We were practicing a hockey stop and something went wrong."

Teresa came over, chattering about not being able to do anything. Dallas was too far toward the middle of the ice for me to get close to him.

He was soon loaded into the ambulance and taken to the hospital five minutes away. I met him there.

He was in some pain but in rather good spirits, enjoying meeting new people and watching them scurrying about to attend to him. He explained what happened.

Lorna had suggested, tactfully, that more mature skaters usually prefer to learn ice dancing moves and routines rather than the jumps and stops of hockey and figure skaters. What would he like to do? Dallas, with buoyancy, said he was willing to go for the hard stuff. She agreed, reluctantly, and demonstrated a hockey stop. Dallas promptly copied but somehow caught the toe of his blade, twisted his foot, and fell. When he looked toward his feet, he saw that his right foot lay limp at a perfect 90 degree angle to his leg. He reached down and twisted it forward, into appropriate position, just before Lorna reached him.

"Are you okay?" she asked.

"My leg is broken," he replied.

"How do you know?" she questioned.

"Believe me, I know."

The paramedics asked the same question, adding, "Are you a doctor?" He just told them to take his word for the reality of the break.

After X-rays, the local bone specialist informed him that the bones were completely snapped a few inches above the ankle, which was not surprising news to Dallas. After consultation, they decided to set the leg and cast it without pins and surgery. It would take longer to heal, but would be stronger. When the deed was done, Dallas was in a cast on his right leg up to his hip. And so ended an active vacation.

I pushed him around in a wheelchair for the remainder of the holiday and we drove back to Utah with him in the back seat, his elevated foot in the front. He called the airline company to request a front seat on the left hand aisle so he could have a place for his plaster cast during the long flight back to Brazil. The full leg cast would stay on until our return to Utah in October for general conference.

Back in Brazil, I drove him to work, to church, and around southern Brazil so he could fulfill his regional representative duties. He became quite competent using crutches, not putting any weight on his right foot, and figuring out ingenious ways to bathe and sleep.

On our return to Salt Lake in October, he saw a doctor who felt surgery should have been performed and suggested he could still do that, but he would have to break the bones again. Dallas decided to continue on the long route. The full leg cast was removed and replaced with a new-fangled Velcro contraption which wrapped around his leg from toes to knee but could be removed to bathe, even to sleep. The only remaining problem was that he still could not put any weight on his right foot. The major challenge in this was that he was always on planes, and most of the airports he went in and out of did not have convenient entry and exit ramps. He usually had to maneuver himself across the tarmac and up and down wobbly aluminum stairs at the doors to the planes, all without touching his right foot to the ground. In spite of the challenges in doing so, this was more fun than riding in a wheelchair.

As I watched all this, I couldn't help but remember other similarly challenging health-related occasions. For example, when he was on his mission in Uruguay he had to have his appendix removed. The most interesting part of the story was that a week after the surgery, the incision became infected and the doctor reopened it without anesthetic and without warning Dallas. As Dallas always said, "He cleaned up the infection, *after* he scraped me off the ceiling." The very next week, "crazy" Dallas and his companion logged almost eighty hours of tracting.

One night in Oakland, we were at Dawn and Clark's for a social evening when Dallas volunteered to run to the corner store to get Dawn a needed quart of milk. When he didn't return in the appropriate amount of time, Clark went after him only to return a few minutes later with Dallas hopping on one foot and hanging on Clark's shoulder. He had slipped on a curb and, examination at the Naval Hospital would later show, had sliced a little bone on the center-side of his foot clean off. During surgery to screw the chipped piece back on, Dallas was awake having been given only local anesthetic. He could hear all the comments as well as the squeak of the screwdriver and screw as his foot was joined back together.

He wore a plaster cast to his knee for a short while until everything seemed fine. But a year later, Dallas could use the feeling in his foot to tell every minor change in the barometer. So the screw was taken out, which decreased but did not eliminate the sensitivity, thereby providing many good opportunities to tell the whole story.

Another time, shortly before departure from the Coast Guard, Dallas took a load of paper to the incinerator to burn. Through the eye level opening, he doused the mass with a little white gas in order to ignite it, but then he waited just a second or two too long before tossing in a match. The resulting explosion sent a whirling ball of fire in his direction. He threw his hands up to cover his face but, when he removed them, they peeled off seared flesh. I was in the bedroom when he ran into the house, grabbed his keys, yelled that he had been burned and was going to the base, and slammed the door on his way out. I did not even see him. But at the base guard station, they refused to let him enter because they didn't recognize him behind the ashen complexion.

He returned home shortly—minus eyebrows, eyelashes, and hairline, his splotchy red face smeared with medicinal grease—though basically none the worse for wear and in reasonably good humor, as usual. He could always see an entertaining story in any challenge. His only concern at that moment was that the base medic might not let him go to Seattle for Seafair. When he began to heal quickly, he cajoled the doctor into believing that he was almost as good as new, and off we went.

Just a couple of years before the Sun Valley broken leg, Dallas had needed surgery for a hernia which was accomplished while on a trip to Utah. His insurance company at the time would not authorize an overnight stay at the hospital; so, he had surgery at 8 a.m., recovered from the anesthesia until about 4 p.m., then we left for my mother's house. I drove as slowly and carefully as I could. Still he insisted that he felt like some cowboy with a gunshot wound in his abdomen, riding off into the sunset. Once at our destination he managed to comfortably settle in but, later that night, a commercial on TV "tickled his funny bone." He started laughing and couldn't stop in spite of the pain it caused. The more he laughed, the more he hurt, and the more he laughed. Soon all of us were laughing with him, hoping his stitches would hold. Thankfully, they did.

Once while on a camp-out where he was trying to establish channels of communication for the Church with leaders of the Boy Scouts of Brazil, he snuck away from the group during an unscheduled moment to do a little fishing. Suddenly he was attacked by a tiny, three-foot tall deer. The deer kept charging him, battering him with its head and trying to bite him. Dallas kept moving away, trying all kinds of evasive maneuvers, but every time he moved the deer would fade back and then charge again. Finally Dallas just took off running back to camp where he decided to check in with the medic. The medic suggested a tetanus shot, which probably was not very useful, but Dallas agreed. Within fifteen minutes Dallas broke out in hives, an apparent reaction to the shot. So, then he went after some medication to control the itching. Later that afternoon, physically uncomfortable, unwilling to try fishing again, and apparently unable to effect the kind of communication necessary with the scout leaders, he packed and left early.

That evening, all the English speaking church members in São Paulo were gathered in a home for a Saturday night social. When Dallas came waltzing in the door, I was surprised since he wasn't suppose to be home until very late. He was still not very comfortable, but he had a really good story—and an audience.

Six months after the Sun Valley ice-skating experience, X-rays showed that the broken leg was healing very slowly, but at least now he could use his right foot in combination with crutches. It would be nine months total before he was free of casts and crutches, and two years before he could skate again.

Finally back on the ice, he told Lorna with a glint in his eye, "I think this would be a good time to take up ice dancing."

He was really a bounce back, beat the odds kind of person—always.

After we had been in Brazil six years, Dallas discovered a piece of paradise that he was able to purchase at a remarkably low price. "The Ranch," as we called it, was located just fifty minutes from our apartment in São Paulo and was a medley of 200 breathtaking Brazilian acres. The hills and dales of the land were often decorated with the purple flowers of lovely *jacarandá* trees. In a valley between the hills, there was a rustic ranch house with a swimming pool, a covered bar-beque pit, and a gigantic picnic table beside a small lake. Frogs croaked, parrots flew through the trees, butterflies of all sizes and colors dipped and swirled about, and hummingbirds fluttered their wings in their trademark way as they drank nectar from innumerable exquisite blossoms. The Garden of Eden could not have been much more elegant than "The Ranch."

Dallas arranged group parties and church camp-outs at The Ranch, thereby utilizing its special advantages for the good of many. All the visiting children followed him around as he taught them about the flora, the fauna, and, of course, the fishing. Dallas got involved in bee-keeping, with all the necessary paraphernalia, and became famous for giving fascinating child-friendly seminars to the fourth grade classes at Teresa's school.

At The Ranch, Dallas and Teresa had a couple of horses and they reveled in the beauty and freedom. It was there that they cemented their very unique Daddy-Daughter connections. They were peas from the same pod and the chemistry between them was just a little bit magic.

Daddy-Daughter Moments

Dallas loved children, all children. He told them stories and, in "Pied Piper" fashion, they followed him everywhere. And he loved his child, his only child. She was the "apple of his eye." When he blessed her at church, he was uncharacteristically precise. Every word was planned and practiced. He was uncomfortable with the structure, but he wanted to be sure and get it right.

When, as a baby, she burned her arm on a pot of hot water, he used the experience as material to illustrate the Atonement. Dallas wanted to be able to take the pain away from her, because she was so vulnerable and because he loved her so. But, of course, he could not. The Savior, however, through His love does have the power to take away our pain.

When she was school age, it was very difficult to get her out of bed in the mornings. Having reached frustration level more than once, Dallas decided it was time for a demonstration. We went out in the street with the car, and Teresa was given an opportunity to try and push it up a small incline—without success. "That's how I feel every morning," Dallas emphasized. "I push you and push you and push you and it doesn't do any good!" Unfortunately, about the only thing seven-year-old Teresa learned from that experience was that it is hard to push a car uphill.

They were so much alike. They were disorderly and impulsive. They liked movement, innovation, verbalizing and socializing. They liked action. They fished and ice-skated and rode horses and played tennis and went camping and skiing. They went to *Aida* and reveled in the majestic, noisy power. He was her softball coach, and he was the wind beneath her wings. They planned ways to go into business together.

Because he believed that "a ship wasn't meant to stay in the harbor," he gave her independence and freedom. When she made mistakes, he forgave her. When he made mistakes, she forgave him.

Often they sat down together to work out her school compositions. Sometimes they sat down together to write one of his presentations. When he needed to compose a paper about families when we were in South America and Teresa was in the United States, they worked together via e-mail. After a few "discussions," he sent her his composition—and she replied.

****

Dear Teri,
Tell me what you think of this:

Believing in children with faith, hope, and charity

Transform the word "faith" into the words "confidence, trust, and respect" and apply them in the daily interaction of the family. Beginning with the parents there must exist complete fidelity as evidenced in the confidence, trust, and respect shown to each other. Parents need to confide, trust, and respect their children and children should do likewise with parents. However, many times children do not show respect to their parents due to being over-structured, over-programmed and over-burdened and because of this, they feel that the parents don't respect them. Over-structuring family goals and programs can deny respect for individuality. Rigidity needs to be replaced with good sense, and commands need to be replaced with questions.

The children need input into family decisions and problems. A family council is a real council and each participant, regardless of age or status, is a council member. Children are not inferior, they just need experience provided by trusting parents in order to understand negotiation and compromise. Much of the help to strengthen the family will come from the innocence of youth as they are included in ways which are joyful and meaningful to them. Confidence, trust and respect in the Savior and Heavenly Father is generated as a family prays, reads scriptures, attends church and serves together. Confidence, trust and respect for the Prophet, general authorities, and local leaders provide an environment of safety and respect for authority.

Hope can be transferred into the word "vision." The family must have the vision of what being sealed together for time and all eternity means. This long range vision must be reduced to short applicable actions of today which will result in worthy temple participation in all stages of life. The complete dot matrix picture of an eternal family requires daily effort in the placing and coloring of each dot by the family. The world wishes to paint a different picture and the dots and colors are different. The vision must be clear.

Transforming the word "charity" into the words love, warmth, and genuine concern gives indication of what must be accomplished in the family. Even Mom and Dad need "warm fuzzies." The example of true and faithful love of the parents for each other radiates through the environment of the home. The extension of that love encompasses the children and brings the family together. Love, warmth, and genuine concern for each member of the family builds self-esteem. Destructive to love and self-esteem is comparative pride. For example, the bumper sticker on a car which reads "proud parents of an honor student" can create competitive pressure and stress which delete the feelings of "love, warmth and genuine" leaving only concern and conflict. True love requires the acceptance of each family member for his or her own special abilities. As the song instructs us, we must "lead, guide and walk beside" a child of God, seeing to it that each is able to do his or her best in comparison with self and not with others.

With the integration of moral agency, there is no "cookbook recipe" which can insure the worthiness of each family member, but without confidence, trust, respect, vision, love, warmth, and genuine concern, the eternal family is at risk. ***

Love, Dad

_____

Dear Dad,

I think your paper is excellent—although it may bother some more conventional minds. I am going to write out some quotes I found in the *Neal A. Maxwell Quote Book* edited by Cory H. Maxwell (Bookcraft; Salt Lake City, Utah; 1997) that you might find useful. I will also point out now, some things that I think may need to be emphasized.

I think that maybe you should mention that to get worthily sealed in the temple as a family, members just need to continue what they are doing: living the commandments—but to enjoy! "There should be less wringing of hands and more loving arms around our families." (p. 118.)

In your second paragraph, when you talk about parents taking away the individuality of the child you might want to add this quote from Maxwell's book, "Though (Satan) postures as a nonconformist, my how the adversary likes his lemmings to line up and march—toward self-destruction—to the most conforming cadence caller of them all!" (p. 61.)

In the fourth paragraph, after "the innocence of youth" you should put the word "also" to clarify that prayer and the following is in combination with councils. Just before you reach the "dot matrix" or at the end of the paragraph you might use this quote: "Those with true hope often see their personal circumstances shaken, like kaleidoscopes, again and again. Yet with the 'eye of faith,' they still see divine pattern and purpose." (p. 164.) And those patterns continue to be what holds a family with vision together.

In your "charity" paragraph, after the example, you might put this quote: "It is possible to have illegitimate pride in a legitimate role or in a deserved reputation. Such pride must go, too, for we are servants of him who lived his unique life as a person of 'no reputation.'" (p. 268.)

I'm going to re-write your last paragraph. "'The human family—without the gospel or without strong families is not going to go very far. Unless we can fix families, you can't fix anything else. Most of the problems that are most vexing are things government can't fix. They have to be fixed at a different level. That's the urgency of our message. I'd rather have ten commandments than ten thousand federal regulations. Unless we rebuild marriages and families, then we are just straightening deck chairs on the Titanic....' (p. 116-117.) There is no 'cookbook recipe' that will ensure the worthiness and salvation of each family member but without confidence, trust, respect, vision, love, warmth, and genuine concern, the eternal family runs an immense risk."

You might want to check through your paper for grammar mistakes. I saw a few. Tell me how it turns out. Have a good day at work!

Love, Teri

****

"Confidence, trust, respect, vision, love, warmth, and genuine concern." Dallas and Teresa had all of those—for each other.

Brazil was a good place for all of us to laugh, to love, to spread our wings and fly. The Brazilian roots of our family were deep and would only grow deeper because of the calling.

THE CALLING

To my knowledge, Dallas never told anyone except me (and twenty years later, Teresa) about his experience with a conference issue of the *Ensign* while we were living in Mexico. He was standing in our extra bedroom—which was at various times the TV room, the guest room, or the nursery—thumbing through the magazine's pages. He stopped to look at a picture of the podium area of the Salt Lake Tabernacle on Temple Square (then the locale for general conference), with its choir seats above the red chairs reserved for general authorities.

Suddenly, he heard or felt the unsummoned words: "Someday you will sit there." He dropped the magazine posthaste and ran, gasping, from the room. Though he had a great singing voice, he knew the message had no reference to the choir seats.

Fourteen years passed.

We had been living in Brazil for almost ten years and were considering the possibility of asking for a transfer in order to be in a location that had more educational options for Teresa. But considering that possibility was as far as we would get.

During the first week in May, 1992, Dallas received a phone call asking him to join the Brazil Area President, Elder Joe J. Christensen, for lunch during a time when we knew Elder Christensen was supposed to be out of town. Elder Christensen was apparently flying back to São Paulo just to have a midday meal with Dallas.

115

We were so curious about the reasons for this unexpected, unexplainable meeting that Dallas called me as soon as lunch was concluded.

"Well?" I asked.

"Nothing!" he replied.

"Nothing?"

"Nothing."

"Then what happened?"

"We had lunch and a nice conversation. He asked a lot of questions, but nothing unusual—except he wanted to know if it would be possible for me to get off work one day a week."

Dallas had been helping the area presidency on some special youth programs and we wondered if they were wanting a little more involvement. Since Dallas was his own boss at the company offices in Brazil and never neglected corporate responsibilities in spite of demanding church callings, one day a week was possible. It also crossed our minds that a new mission president who already had a Brazilian visa might be needed, although nothing in the conversation indicated such a vacancy.

Feeling that something in our lives might change, we put a few plans on hold. One week went by, then two weeks with no further mention from the authorities of the lunchtime conversation. Therefore, during the third week in May we halted our curiosity and put life back on track with a commitment to stay in Brazil at least one more year.

Dallas, unlike me, was an early riser. On the morning of May 29, at 6 a.m., he came in the bedroom after his personal scripture study time and gently woke me up.

"I know what's going on," he whispered.

"About what?" I mumbled.

"About the lunch conversation with Elder Christensen." I was suddenly awake, interested.

"What about it?" I queried, trying to focus my eyes.

He grinned one of those, "I'm so clever" kinds of grins. "I was in the living room studying just now and it came to me. Remember in Spain when we talked about how the Church needed to ask some seasoned Priesthood leaders to work overseas so they could be called upon to assist the Seventies in international areas?"

I nodded. When we were in Spain we were part of the Europe West Area, a large area which included several different countries and languages. Our direct supervisor was a member of the Quorum of the Seventy who served as an Area Executive Administrator, alone, without counselors. We never knew how he was able to do all he was required to do. We thought some leaders who would continue in their own occupations should be asked to live abroad, if not already doing so, and be called as counselors. A few years later, the area presidency concept came into being and our idea seemed moot and academic.

"Well," Dallas went on, "they are going to do it. They are going to call someone to be a general authority and ask him to keep his job. And I'm it."

"Really?" I hardly knew what to say.

"Really. I just know."

He left nothing for me to question or to say at that particular moment.

Later that afternoon, at 4:30 p.m., Dallas was at the NCH office. The phone rang.

"*Senhor Dallas*," his secretary called. "*Os Estados Unidos está ligando.*" (Mr. Dallas, the United States is calling.)

Dallas waved at her and replied, "*Eu sei.*" (I know.)

Unlike that telephone call asking him to serve as mission president when he was scarcely able to breathe, this time he sat back and relaxed, even put his feet up on the desk and picked up the receiver.

It was President Gordon B. Hinckley, then a counselor in the First Presidency.

After the appropriate greetings, President Hinckley said that he had been with the brethren and they were unanimous in issuing Dallas a call to serve as a general authority. However, he explained, this call would be different than any before. He would be a general authority with all authority and responsibilities, but he would also keep his job. There would be no compensation or benefits from the Church except travel expenses.

They discussed details for a few minutes, then President Hinckley asked Dallas if he thought this new system would work.

Dallas paused for a second. I'm sure a smile crept across his face as he contemplated the stunned surprise his reply would produce.

"Yes, President, I do. In fact, I discussed it with my wife this morning."

Then, of course, he had to explain the morning moment of personal revelation.

Dallas was called to the Second Quorum of the Seventy which meant he would serve as a general authority for five years. And he was called as second counselor in the Brazil Area Presidency with President Harold G. Hillam and Elder Helvecio Martins. Under the direction of the Quorum of the Twelve Apostles, an area presidency supervises all church work, including mission presidents and missionary work, in a particular area. One other new member of the Quorum of the Seventy was called to the same program as Dallas: Elder Augusto Lim of the Philippines. Twenty-five years earlier, Dallas and Elder Lim had been home teaching companions in Manila.

Brazil is huge, approximately the size of the United States, and church growth was about to explode. The demands of a full-time job and a full-time calling would tax Dallas's time tremendously. But there were some who said it wasn't really fair to use him in the pilot project because he was the original "Energizer Bunny" who never stops.

Everyone knew that he could "change hats" effectively as he juggled offices and duties and still, somehow, keep the pace.

Two months after the phone call from President Hinckley, Dallas received a letter asking him to speak at the Saturday afternoon session of October General Conference. So now, when he was at home, he was hunched over the computer working out his discourse. He told me later that he felt the rough draft was given to him by inspiration. He knew from the beginning what he was supposed to talk about. The time he spent working with the text was to refine it, become extremely familiar with it in order to fit it into nine minutes and not be intimidated by the Teleprompter.

On Saturday, October 3, 1992, the day he was to speak, he took a short lunch and long shower alone in our hotel room between the morning and afternoon sessions of conference. He seemed nervous, and friends later commented that he appeared tense as he spoke. "It must be difficult to speak in the Tabernacle," they consoled. But I knew that, for Dallas, the Tabernacle posed no problem. He could always captivate an audience; and he could speak to multitudes, including a TV audience and a forum of authorities, from any podium in any location for hours if necessary and never be tense—as long as he didn't have to follow a precise script and fit his remarks into an exact time limit. Because he was spontaneity personified, the structure made him feel uneasy.

I actually felt quite peaceful as he began to speak. Everything seemed natural. I had heard him speak so often in so many places. But then, suddenly, his name flashed across the bottom of the TV screen on the monitor located in front of the area were I was sitting: *Elder Dallas N. Archibald, Quorum of Seventy.* The reality hit me with some pain and drew tears. *How did this happen? What did we think we were doing? We didn't belong here!* Then, just as quickly, I realized that with God nothing is impossible. I was very grateful to be married to Elder Dallas N. Archibald, Quorum of Seventy.

A few days later, I wrote him a note: "Thanks for the incredible journey." But that afternoon in the Tabernacle, I just fetched a tissue from my handbag and listened to his message which, I knew, came straight from his heart.

Born of Goodly Parents
Elder Dallas N. Archibald, of the Seventy

Recently, I had the opportunity to sit at the back of a chapel during a sharing time session of Primary and watch a lively group of youngsters keep a music teacher very busy. For a final song the director asked the children to sing "I Am a Child of God." They quieted down, and for the first song of the entire session the voices unified in quality instead of quantity. The words rang throughout the chapel with an angel-like resonance:

Lead me, guide me, walk beside me,
Help me find the way.
Teach me all that I must do
To live with him someday.
(*Hymns*, 1985, 301)

These pleading words sank deep into my heart that day and stirred my soul. What a great burden of responsibility the Lord has placed upon us as parents: to take these children and lead them in the ways of holiness, to guide them through the perils of mortality, and to walk beside them on the straight and narrow path which leads to eternity. Yes, the responsibility is ours to teach them all they must do so that, someday as the mortal is changed to immortal, they will be prepared to return to the presence of the Father and dwell with him and their Elder Brother, Jesus Christ.

The Book of Mormon clearly shows the value of righteousness and dedication in parents. The first statement of Nephi is a tribute to his parents: "I, Nephi, having been born of goodly parents, therefore I was taught somewhat in all the learning of my father." (1 Ne. 1:1.) Enos wrote, "And the words which I had often heard my father speak concerning eternal life, and the joy of the saints, sunk deep into my heart." (Enos 1:3.) Mormon recorded of Nephi and Lehi, the two sons of Helaman: "For they remembered the words which their father Helaman spake unto them. And these are the words which he spake." (Hel.5:5.) Here we have a tribute to a goodly parent and also the words which he spoke to his children. He reminded them of the names he had given them so that they would always seek to do good works and desire the precious gift of eternal life. (See vs. 6-7.) Then he told them, "O remember, remember, my sons, the words which King Benjamin spake unto his people; yea, remember that there is no other way nor means whereby man can be saved, only through the atoning blood of Jesus Christ." (v.9.)

The reference to the words of King Benjamin shows that Helaman, as a parent, knew the scriptures and taught his children to follow the words of the prophets. He continued, saying, "And now, my sons, remember, remember that it is upon the rock of our Redeemer, who is Christ, the Son of God, that ye must build your foundation."(v. 12.)

What better teaching could a parent provide for a child than that of following the prophets and building a sure foundation upon Jesus Christ? The Book of Mormon prophet Jacob instructed that once they have been taught and "obtained a hope in Christ," we may then teach them how to earn riches so that they can use them "to clothe the naked, and to feed the hungry." (Jacob 2:18-19.) We must teach them all that they must do to live with Him, and the best teacher is example.

As I sat there in the back of the chapel, I silently asked myself, "Am I doing all the things which I must do? Can my wife and daughter walk alongside me with confidence that I will lead them into the celestial kingdom? 'Lead me, guide me, walk beside me...'" Stop. Stop for one minute, and ask the same question of yourself: "Can my spouse and children walk alongside me with confidence that I will lead them into the celestial kingdom?" The Savior said, "Seek ye first the kingdom of God." (Matt. 6:33.)

The instructions are clear. We must teach, and we must be an example of those teachings; but many times in our zeal to persuade others to righteousness we begin to use force, which results in rebellion. Attempting to force others to accept our way of thinking will cause them to close their minds to our teachings and ultimately reject our words. They have their free agency.

In the Doctrine and Covenants, Section 121, the Lord explains the proper way to teach. He said, "Only by persuasion, by long-suffering, by gentleness and meekness, and by love unfeigned;

"By kindness, and pure knowledge, which shall greatly enlarge the soul." (v. 41-42.) How I love those words "enlarge the soul." Proper teaching will enlarge the soul.

For example, let us compare a child to an empty glass, and our knowledge and experience, which have accumulated over the years, to a bucketful of water. Logic and physics tell us that we cannot pour a bucketful of water directly into a small glass. However, by using correct principles of transferring knowledge, the glass can be enlarged. Those principles are persuasion, long-suffering, gentleness and meekness, love unfeigned, kindness, and pure knowledge. They will enlarge the glass, which is the soul of the child, allowing that child to receive much more than the original bucketful.

Behavioral psychologists have written libraries of books upon this subject. The Lord gave us the same information in just a few verses of scripture. We must always teach, lead, and guide in a way which will create high levels of self-esteem in our children and others.

To create and maintain self-esteem, our words and our actions must always express to the individual that he or she is important and capable. The words the scriptures use are "to lift." The psychologists would say, "Reinforce the positive." The secret is simple. Always look for the good in the individual and lift, reinforce the positive by words and actions. Put-downs, words like "stupid" or "dummy," or phrases like "Why can't you do anything right?" destroy self-esteem and shouldn't be part of our vocabulary. It is impossible to emphasize the good in others if negative words or phrases are readily available on the tips of our tongues or expressed through our gestures.

The plea behind the words "walk beside me, help me find the way" is this: "Lift me. Strengthen my feeble knees. Let me know that I am important and capable." (See D&C 81:5.)

When correction and discipline must take place, it is essential to continue lifting and strengthening, ensuring that the feelings of being important and capable are not lost. Again, in section 121 of the Doctrine and Covenants, the Lord explains how: "Reproving betimes with sharpness, when moved upon by the Holy Ghost; and then showing forth afterwards an increase of love toward him whom thou hast reproved." (v. 43.)

As Elder Maxwell has observed, the word betimes is casually assumed to mean "from time to time," or "occasionally," when actually it means "early on." Therefore, correction must take place early on with the direction of the Holy Ghost and not in anger. One hundred and thirty-two years ago, in a discourse in this tabernacle, Brigham Young counseled, "Never chasten beyond the balm you have within you to bind up." (*Journal of Discourses*, 9:124-25.) The Lord said, "...showing forth afterward an increase of love." (D&C 121:43.)

The instructions on how to correct are clear and simple: early on, with the peace of the Holy Ghost, and with enough of the healing power within us to make sure that self-esteem is never wounded, ensuring always that the individual feels important and capable.

Oh, goodly parent, hear the words and respond accordingly:

Lead me, guide me, walk beside me,
    Help me find the way.
Teach me all that I must do
    To live with him someday.

In the holy name of Jesus Christ, amen.

(© by Intellectual Reserve, Inc.; Previously published in the *Ensign* magazine; November 1992; 25-26; used by permission.)

Dallas felt a particular affinity for the children and the youth of the Church. Across the United States and around the world he worked mightily to teach respect for them and to establish programs which would strengthen them. In Brazil, in large measure through his efforts and the facilities at The Ranch, young men and young women camp programs were established which became the core of youth activities, a missionary tool, and a powerful source of testimony building. At appropriate times, he spoke to them frankly about the discipline needed to avoid the ever-present temptations and moral decay in today's society.

He also worked with the area presidency to teach missionaries more effective ways of communicating with fathers in order to bring whole families together to Christ, and to encourage members to make the effort to receive the blessings of the temple with their families. The temple in São Paulo was six days distance of day and night travel for some members in some cities in the north. Yet, members often sold all they had and took boats and buses, sometimes standing most of the journey, arriving after almost a week of continuous travel. Then they would disembark, weary and worn, and reverently gravitate in the direction of the temple where they would, with their children, reach out and gently touch the temple walls. After a week of temple work, they would board the buses and boats and return home, radiant, ready to rebuild their temporal lives. Dallas, with emotion in his voice, always commended and honored their sacrifice.

Speaking at stake conferences was always one of his favorite things. Sometimes he was acutely aware of the power of inspiration:

—In the morning session of a stake conference in São Paulo (half the stake met in the morning, the other half in the afternoon), Dallas decided to fill up a little extra time by having the stake president ask a young woman on the front row to spontaneously bear her testimony, which she did beautifully. He intended to spontaneously call on another young woman in the afternoon session, and noticed a young girl entering the hall at the beginning of the meeting who became his potential candidate. However, as the meeting progressed, time was filled up and there were no extra minutes prior to Dallas's section at the end of the meeting. Therefore, he notified the stake president to eliminate the testimony from the schedule.

Nevertheless, as Dallas began speaking, he again noticed the previously identified girl in the congregation and again felt impressed to ask her to bear her testimony, which he immediately did. The young woman tearfully approached the pulpit and bore a short and sweet witness of her faith.

As she was speaking, her mother penned a quick note to the stake president. "Did President Archibald arrange this in advance?" she asked. Then she explained that as the family ate lunch before leaving for conference, her daughter had said, "When President Archibald asks me to speak this afternoon, I will cry."

—Dallas was speaking in the final segment of a stake conference in tropical Recife, Brazil. As he began to sum up his remarks, he looked at his watch and noticed that he would be finishing a few minutes early. He had a small impression to speak about a different subject, but dismissed it believing that the congregation would appreciate an early release on this warm day. As he started to conclude, however, the overhead fan in the room ruffled the pages of his scriptures and turned them to a chapter where the topic of the small impression was discussed. Not requiring a third notification to understand that he was supposed to speak about that subject, he launched into a brief presentation knowing this would take the meeting slightly overtime.

After he had finally concluded and the prayer had been said, as he was gathering up his books and papers, a woman came quickly toward him from the back of the chapel calling his name. "Oh, Elder Archibald. Thank you." She was smiling through her tears. "I came here today fasting and praying for an answer to a personal problem, and when I saw you begin to finish your talk, I thought I would have to look elsewhere for answers. But then you looked down at your scriptures, and everything you said after that was exactly what I needed to hear."

For me, there is one moment from those years indelibly printed in my mind. It occurred on a trip to Utah when Dallas was invited to perform the marriage of the daughter of good friends of ours in the Logan Temple. Upon arrival at the temple, Dallas went to change into his white suit while I mingled with the family and went on with them to the sealing room. As we sat waiting, Dallas suddenly stepped through the doorway catching me by surprise—and my heart skipped a beat. In his white suit, he looked very adorable and very official.

126

The bride and groom, Annette and Ryan, soon joined us in the sealing room. Dallas had worked long hours to prepare his instructions for them—drawing, I was sure, on his own marriage experiences for counsel. His short message of advice couldn't have been better. The ceremony was heartfelt; and I was captivated completely, one more time, so glad I was his and he was mine.

After three years in his combined assignment of full-time temporal and spiritual duties, the general authority pilot program was revised. Many Area Authority Seventies were called to serve as Dallas had done: in particular geographical areas while also remaining in their professions. They would work with area presidencies and were called to the third, fourth, and fifth quorums of the Seventy. Dallas was then called to be the area president in Brazil, a responsibility which was more than a full-time job. Now he would have to retire from NCH.

The twenty-four years with the company had been fantastic. Dallas had done his best for them and they had supported him in marvelous ways, even during the three years in Spain and the three years he had served in his double-duty general authority responsibilities. We felt that Dallas had been impressed, back in graduate school, to join the NCH team because they would give us such outstanding assistance over the years. We would always think of them as our friends, and the feeling was mutual. The corporate directors, Lester, Milton and Irvin Levy wrote: "Dallas, you have earned a place of trust, respect and honor in our hearts. This feeling is shared with Keith and with everyone in the company with whom you work. You are a man of excellent business ability—more than that, you are a man of sterling character." We knew that we would sincerely miss their close association.

In Brazil, Dallas settled into full-time church work—and there was plenty of that. As area president, he was just as busy as when he had two full-time jobs; but, as a second quorum member, he had only two years remaining of his five-year call. We did not know what we would do when that time ended. There was a good possibility that we would decide to stay in Brazil for a couple of years. However, just in case we did not choose that option, the week before April conference 1996 we called Jeff and Barbara Marchant, our friends from the Arizona days, and asked them to gather some information for us on real estate in their home town of Cedar City, Utah. But the very next week we had to call them and repeal our request when Dallas was called to the First Quorum of the Seventy making him a general authority until the age of 70—twelve more years.

Though our future was now subject to change at any summons from the brethren, we knew we had at least one more year in Brazil and we tried to enjoy it to the fullest. We assumed that since we had been overseas for so long, our next assignment would be to church headquarters in Salt Lake City. Therefore, we were surprised at April conference 1997 when we were advised of a transfer to Santiago, Chile. From Brazil, Dallas had supervised the work for NCH in Chile and he loved the place and the people. Though we would have to leave Brazil, thoughts of Chile relieved the pain.

So many good things had happened in Brazil. We had seen the Church grow from 6 missions to 26, from 30 stakes to almost 200. Teresa was four years old when we arrived. Now she was nineteen. The roots were very deep and goodbyes were melancholy, especially with the sale of our piece of paradise, The Ranch. But Chile was a continuation of the work where Dallas would use the same effective techniques that had served him so well in Brazil.

The Tapestry

For many years, we used frequent flier miles to travel from Brazil to Utah for a week at Christmastime. In order to make this a free trip all the way from São Paulo to Salt Lake, we had to go through Kennedy Airport in New York City. We arrived there about 7 a.m. and our plane to Salt Lake did not leave until 5 p.m. that evening. We were members of one of the airline clubs and usually spent the day in the lounge reading and watching TV, with occasional strolls around the airport. At least that is what we did when all three of us were together.

One year Teresa and I flew to Utah in mid-December and Dallas followed a couple of days before Christmas. He was too restless to sit at the New York airport alone, so he took a bus into the city with no special plans in mind. He began wandering down Fifth Avenue looking, he said, for a Christmas present for me. We had some extra money that year from some good investments, and (since I wasn't around to stop him) he planned to spend it.

Passing by a rather elegant looking jewelry store, he entered and began browsing. The store had just opened for the day and, in accordance with cultural traditions, the middle eastern proprietor was anxious to bring good luck to the day by making an early sale through kind and courteous persuasion. Dallas was a good salesman and a good customer. He had time to kill and, therefore, could easily keep the salesman involved for hours in friendly but purposeful conversation.

They looked at length at jewelry selections but, as Brazil is the paradise of gemstones, Dallas saw nothing in New York which exceeded things back home. After a bit of chit-chat, Dallas was deciding to move on and look elsewhere when the salesman suggested they examine some specialty items on the second floor.

Most of the second floor inventory was Persian rugs. Dallas was fascinated with the merchandise and spent some time being taught by the proprietor about the history, the textiles, and the weaving process even though he had no intention to buy. Finally he explained that he wasn't interested in taking a rug to Brazil, wasn't interested in a purchase.

The salesman was apparently determined to make a good luck sale.

"Come over here," he motioned, drawing Dallas toward a corner of the room. "I have something special I want to show you." Dallas followed, obediently.

The salesman opened a small chest and took from it a rolled tapestry. "This is a silk, hand-tied Hereke," and he explained the weaving technique and history. He showed Dallas the weave and the knots and the colors. He rolled out the 4' x 6' work of art and described the design. "Here is depicted the tree of life," he said, and Dallas pricked up his ears. "See the tree and the fruit and the birds." The design was very nice—beige and pink and a touch of green. Dallas was tempted and so indicated. "But…" he began to retreat.

Just then, the salesman turned the tapestry over—over to the top side. Dallas had been looking at the bottom, the underside. If the bottom with its pastels had been nice, this scene was exquisite. The birds and trees in pink and silver and pale green appeared cast in velvet, and the entire background glistened with gold. Dallas stood back, awed, speechless. Finally he reached out and touched it, ever so carefully. The salesman waited, quietly.

Dallas surveyed the art from every angle. He was converted. He asked for the salesman's best price, and was given an offer he couldn't refuse.

He hand-carried the tapestry to Utah and then he carried it around to every holiday party we went to in order to tell the story, as it happened, and watch the rapt expressions on the faces of his listeners as he concluded by turning the tapestry over, just as the salesman had done, to display the elegance of the upper side.

Following that Christmas season, Dallas often used the story of the tapestry as a teaching tool. His words, however, did not explain textiles and techniques. Rather they illustrated the worth of souls: "Just as I first saw only the incomplete underside of the tapestry, we see only the incomplete mortal nature of our lives. If everyone, all the children of our Father in Heaven, could but see the upper side, the complete picture, we would then see ourselves as He does and we would know that each of us is exquisite, elegant, and unique. We would be able to see our eternal worth: the velvet and the silver and the gold."

Like a Velveteen Rabbit

In Brazil, I was once asked to speak to a group of missionaries about the importance of studying the scriptures. As a seminary and gospel doctrine teacher, I was fairly comfortable with the subject and so I prepared a presentation of techniques for studying and marking along with an overview of some interesting scriptural topics. When that part was organized, however, I felt that I needed a creative way to try and help my students understand what it means to love the scriptures and feast upon the words of Christ. For several days, I pondered and prayed, trying to come up with an idea.

The morning of the day I was to speak, I noticed Dallas's Portuguese scriptures lying on a chair in the living room. He had taught from them in countless classes and meetings as well as having used them to learn gospel vocabulary in Portuguese after we arrived in Brazil. They had brown zipper covers but the covers were spotted, scratched, and discolored and the zippers no longer worked. Inside, some pages were loose and falling out. Hundreds of notes and references were written in tiny print in the margins. Many verses were marked, underlined, circled, and cross-referenced. At various intervals newspaper clippings, charts, and extra pages on which he had written stories, summaries, and other data were glued to the internal margin providing supplementary material which he used during speeches and other presentations.

As I looked at his tattered and torn books, I caught a vision of how to end my speech. I picked them up and took them with me. At the conclusion of my talk, I told the story of *The Velveteen Rabbit* (by Margery Williams, Avon Books, New York, 1982).

"Once upon a time," I said, "a little boy was given a beautiful velveteen rabbit. He was a fat, fluffy rabbit, brown and white, with whiskers. And the boy loved the velveteen rabbit. He played with the rabbit, and snuggled with him, and slept with him. The rabbit went everywhere with the boy, and he was very happy—so happy that he didn't realize his fur was getting shabby, and his seams were coming apart, and the pink of his nose was fading because that was where the boy always kissed him.

"Time passed. Even though the rabbit became very old and worn, the boy still loved him. The rabbit's colors faded, and he wasn't fat and fluffy any more. But to the boy, he was still beautiful and that was all that mattered."

At this point, I held up Dallas's scriptures. I displayed the worn covers, broken zippers, and misshapen forms. I opened the books to reveal the loose pages as well as the many markings, writings, and inserts. Then I recounted the end of the story of the Velveteen Rabbit, how one day, in spite of—or more accurately because of—his dilapidated state, the rabbit became a Real Rabbit, a living rabbit, because he had been so loved by the boy.

"These books," I concluded, "like the rabbit, were originally very splendid; but now the finish has been worn off the covers from being constantly carried about, the zippers are broken, and the pages have deteriorated from constant use. But, believe me, they are loved. When we love our scriptures this way, in the same way that the boy loved the velveteen rabbit, they will one day become Real, a living thing, alive and beautiful."

Dallas eventually got a new set of Portuguese scriptures, but they soon looked almost as tattered and torn as the first set. And, of course, he had a Spanish set and an English set, too. He loved them all. They all became "living scriptures."

Money Matters

Dallas relished opportunities to teach others about financial management. He was, truly, a businessman at heart. In Spain, he taught the missionaries about budgeting their money. One missionary actually became converted to the gospel and to missionary work through the discipline of learning to budget. In Brazil and Chile, Dallas often called meetings and arranged firesides where he could share perspectives on money, budgeting, and investing. He believed totally in Jacob's teachings on riches in *The Book of Mormon*—and, in his rather flamboyant way, he set out to convince others.

"Think of your brethren like unto yourselves, and be familiar with all and free with your substance, that they may be rich like unto you.

"But before ye seek for riches, seek ye for the kingdom of God.

"And after ye have obtained a hope in Christ ye shall obtain riches, if ye seek them; and ye will seek them for the intent to do good—to clothe the naked, and to feed the hungry, and to liberate the captive, and administer relief to the sick and the afflicted."

(Jacob 2:17-19)

He told them about our financially slim days in California and Utah and Arizona and the Philippines, etc., how we planned ahead for even small purchases, and how we often did without until we had enough available funds.

133

He taught them how to sacrifice and save in order to get a return on their investment which would allow them future security. He gave them vision and opened their eyes to possibilities.

And he told them that there are laws of money that, if followed, would allow them to move up on the financial scale.

He did not tell them that he followed Jacob's advice about caring for others; nevertheless he did—countless times, in countless different ways. But he did often tell a story, a true story, to illustrate that financial success can belong to anyone who has sufficient vision and desire. He told them about his search for ways to help members in financial distress, and about the family who helped him understand how to explain the rules.

****

He had been standing motionless for some time watching the droplets of water run down the window distorting, blurring, and magnifying the distant neon lights. With his hands in a rest position behind his back from a habit picked up during military service years before, his body was still though his mind was fully engaged and straining like a finely-tuned automobile against a steep hill. He was used to solving problems with instantaneous decisions and his business success was a result of being able to select the better solution most of the time. He had learned as a missionary that if a person really strived to keep his life in harmony with gospel principles, the Lord would take him by the hand and lead him.

At graduate school, the business teachers said that the conclusion of a decision-making process was often accompanied by a "gut feeling" of certainty. He knew this feeling as the confirmation of the Spirit that came after the necessary initial work had been realized. For him to pray twenty to thirty times during an average working day for this confirmation process was not just habit but also a burning desire within him to know the will of God in temporal as well as spiritual affairs, and God had blessed him with many of his heart's desires.

The problem now facing him was not one which could be resolved instantly. Every mental avenue he followed quickly became a dead end or ran into a road block as it was weighed against the norms. Somehow, someway, a positive and correct action could be taken and only a little more creative thinking was needed to find the solution. Back to square one and start over again.

Square one was a leadership meeting he had participated in a few days before when many of the local leaders had mentioned the high unemployment rate and the financial difficulties of so many members. Dreams and visions seemed futile because of the abject poverty of so many.

The needs were so great. The resources so limited. He felt the muscles along the front of his throat tighten, a slight increase of water in his eyes, and a sinking feeling in the pit of his stomach. He felt as though he were witnessing a forest fire rip through a sacred grove of trees and all that was available to quench the flames was a glass of water. But then, perhaps it wasn't for this current generation to receive the temporal benefits that can accompany spiritual growth.

As he pondered, he remembered a family he knew in another area of the world who had joined the Church. The local members had criticized the missionaries who baptized this family from "down by the river." There were several small children, and the father and mother had built their home with cardboard boxes for walls and five gallon tin cans flattened out for a roof to keep off the wet season rains. The clothes they wore to church were clean but threadbare and patched over and over again with non-matching cloth and hand-stitching. Many members thought that this family would never attend meetings following their baptism, while others speculated about how much time would pass before they were at the bishop's office looking for welfare.

But the family did come to the meetings, and they did not request welfare assistance.

For years, this family was one of the first to arrive at the chapel on Sunday mornings and Mom and Dad would take the children through the building to teach and train. "—This is a carpet. We don't have a carpet at home but here you will learn how to take care of one because someday you will have a home of your own with a carpet and you will need to know how to keep it clean. Wipe your feet first outside on the little mat." "—This is a toilet with self-contained water. Learn how to use it because someday you'll have one in your own home. Smell how clean this bathroom is. Watch what they do to keep it clean because someday, when you have a bathroom like this, you will have to keep it fresh and sanitary."

Kitchen, walls, floors, windows, and garden. All this was taught at church because of the example of a well-maintained chapel. At home the cardboard walls were painted with inexpensive white, powdery paint and the dirt floors were packed hard and cleaned until an observer could see them shine. A garden was grown giving practical beauty as well as strength to young growing bodies. But more than anything else there was hope, a vision that life had more to offer and that, through their faith in God and themselves, they were continually preparing to take full advantage of each opportunity.

For a living, the father collected cardboard boxes from behind stores and out of garbage bins. These he opened and spread out flat before stacking them on a hand-drawn cart which looked something like the handcarts the pioneers had used to cross the plains, except he had used an old car axle and rubber tires for the base. Throughout the day and late into each night, he would stack the discovered cardboard into the cart and then, with his thin wiry frame, arch his back into the task of pushing and pulling his load to a depository where it was weighed and a meager amount of money placed into his cracked, calloused, and sometimes bleeding hands. Arriving at home, the family would immediately meet together to allocate where the money was to be spent.

First was tithing and then a little for fast offerings. Financial obligations to the Lord were the priority. The next priority was ten percent paid into savings for missions for the boys and for education for all the children. The family called these savings their "golden future." The few coins left were used for daily living, even if daily living was bread and water for the parents and a little milk for the children. Somehow they had learned the elementary laws of money as well as the discipline required to receive the reciprocal blessings.

The routine never changed even as the years passed by. The faith and hope established at home and fortified by church auxiliary programs built strong, capable youth. As a result of tremendous sacrifice, in a journey equivalent to crossing the plains, temple blessings were received and the family was sealed together for time and all eternity.

The "golden years" had begun.

When the children were old enough to work, all funds of the family were combined. Missions were served and educational goals achieved until each child had graduated from college and pursued chosen vocations. One was a medical doctor, another a teacher, another a lawyer. Because of the financial discipline accrued through the years of training from their parents, the children rapidly combined their resources and were able to purchase a piece of land with a small furnished house for their parents—a house away from the "river," a house with carpets, and a bathroom with fixtures and running water, a kitchen with a stove, sink, refrigerator and ample cabinets stocked with cans and boxes of food. It was a house the parents had envisioned for their children but never had expected for themselves.

Standing by the window, remembering this family, Dallas knew the answer he had been seeking. He could not change the circumstances of the local members from without, but he could teach the principles of financial discipline used by this family. He would teach and, if they chose to follow, the members would then be able to govern themselves and change from within.

"And after ye have obtained a hope in Christ ye shall obtain riches, if ye seek them; and ye will seek them for the intent to do good..."

Love is the Answer

(The following stories are from unknown sources. I either heard Dallas tell them or found them among his papers without reference or author. I know only that he loved them.)

Dallas didn't use the word "love" often, but he told stories about it all the time. He was a master at stirring emotions. He told short stories and long stories. He told brand new stories and time-worn tales. He told first person stories and re-told stories. He told any story he could find that would reach into the hearts of his audience and turn on the emotional tap of tears. In the back of his Spanish *Book of Mormon*, he had even inserted a newspaper article on the therapeutic value of emotion and sensitivity. It was titled "Is Society Ready for Men Who Cry?" (*Deseret News*, Friday, April 12, 1996). Perhaps he glanced at that article, briefly, every time he left the pulpit with a damp handkerchief in hand.

He knew that love was the antidote to most of society's ills. If people could just learn to be more sensitive, more considerate of others, then kindness would replace cruelty, concern would replace apathy, and caring and sharing would replace competing and comparing.

138

He often spoke of the challenges that exist in community living: "During the glacial age, many animals died because of the cold. The porcupines, understanding the situation, resolved to join in a group and, in this way, cover and protect each other. But the quills of each porcupine wounded their closest companions, those that were actually giving them the most warmth. For this reason, the group separated. But then they realized that they needed to make a choice: disappear from the face of the earth or accept the quills of their neighbor. With wisdom, they decided to return and stay together, learning to live with the small wounds that a very close relationship can cause but realizing that the most important thing is the warmth received from others."

Dallas was something of an expert on porcupines after so many years living with me, and he knew that learning to live together in love was worth the effort. "Sacrifice your own interests when appropriate," he taught, "in order to value and validate another." In this context, he often told the story of Brazilian Emperor Dom Pedro II and Dona Teresa.

"D. Pedro, the second Brazilian Emperor, had grown up in Brazil; but when he was old enough to wed, an emissary was sent to Europe, as was the custom, to find a wife from among the royal families. Because Brazil was so far away, no young woman was found who wished to wed D. Pedro II—until Teresa, a homely and slightly handicapped princess of Naples, Italy volunteered.

"Because the search for a bride had been so difficult, at this point the emissary decided to take matters into his own hands. He had Teresa's picture 'touched up' in order to camouflage her homeliness and handicaps and sent it to D. Pedro, who, being duly impressed with what he saw, readily agreed to the union.

"The wedding was actually conducted in Europe with a proxy standing in for D. Pedro, and an informal ceremony and elegant reception was planned for Brazil.

"On the beach in Rio de Janeiro, the bridegroom waited anxiously for the arrival of Teresa but, when she disembarked from the ship, he was confused and dismayed. During the ride from the docks to the palace he wondered what to do, and more than once the thought surfaced, 'It will be difficult to remain faithful.' But to D. Pedro those words were uncomfortable, in conflict with his personal integrity.

"When he arrived at the palace, he began a long day and night of personal soul-searching as well as considerable discussion with trusted associates. By morning, after a sleepless night, he had made his decision. The wedding would be fully validated and he would be faithful.

"After that a miracle happened as D. Pedro and Teresa fell in love with each other, and together found common love in history, art, literature, in their two children and in Brazil. D. Pedro had never known another country and Teresa accepted Brazil as her native land. D. Pedro traveled extensively throughout the western hemisphere, even visiting Salt Lake City and writing of his positive impressions of the place and the people.

"When D. Pedro and Teresa were older, on a November day, messengers came to them. The people, they said, no longer wanted a monarch. They wanted to be a republic, the wave of the future. D. Pedro replied that if this was truly the will of the people, he would not stand in their way; but, in that event, he could not remain in Brazil.

"A few days later, as he and Teresa prepared to board the ship for Europe, she stopped at the foot of the gangplank and sadly scooped up a handful of Brazilian soil so she would have something of her beloved Brazil to take with her.

"A few weeks after arriving in Europe, Teresa became ill and passed away. A very short time after that D. Pedro also died. Although advanced age, arduous travel, and physiological weaknesses must be considered, it was said among the people that she could not live without Brazil, and he could not live without her."

Besides brotherly love and family love, Dallas often spoke of gospel love. Whenever a choir or congregation sang the hymn "How Great Thou Art," his handkerchief was out before he ever reached the pulpit: "And when I think that God, his Son not sparing; sent Him to die, I scare can take it in, that on the cross my burden gladly bearing He bled and died to take away my sin." (*Hymns, 86.*) And then he spoke of the incomparable love in the Atonement: "An article in *National Geographic* several years ago provided a penetrating picture of God's wings. After a forest fire in Yellowstone National Park, forest rangers began their trek up a mountain to assess the inferno's damage. One ranger found a bird literally petrified in ashes, perched statuesquely on the ground at the base of a tree.

"Somewhat sickened by the eerie sight, he knocked over the bird with a stick. When he struck it, three tiny chicks scurried from under their dead mother's wings. The loving mother, keenly aware of impending disaster, had carried her offspring to the base of the tree and had gathered them under her wings, instinctively knowing that the toxic smoke would rise. She could have flown to safety but had refused to abandon her babies. When the blaze had arrived and the heat had singed her small body, the mother had remained steadfast. Because she had been willing to die, those under the cover of her wings would live.

"He shall cover thee with his feathers, and under his wings shalt thou trust" (Ps. 91:4).

Often Dallas would follow such poignant teaching with a re-told story, illustrating how our hearts should turn to the Savior's sacrifice when partaking of the sacrament: "The Sacrament never really meant much to me until the Sunday I was ordained a deacon. That afternoon I passed the sacrament for the first time. Prior to the meeting, one of the deacons warned me, 'Look out for Brother Schmidt. You may have to wake him up!'

"Finally the time came for me to participate in the passing of the sacrament. I handled the first six rows quite well. Children and adults partook of the bread with no noticeable thought or problem. Then I got to row seven, to the row where Brother Schmidt always sat. But I was surprised. Instead of being asleep, he was wide awake. Unlike many of the others I had served, he took the bread with what seemed to be great thought and reverence.

"A few minutes later I found myself again approaching row seven with the water. This time my friend was right. Brother Schmidt sat with his head bowed and his big German eyes shut. He was evidently sound asleep. What could I do or say? I looked for a moment at his brow, wrinkled and worn from years of toil and hardship. He had joined the Church as a teenager and had experienced much persecution in his small German town. I had heard the story many times in testimony meeting.

"I decided finally to gently nudge his shoulder in hopes of waking him. As I reached to do so, his head slowly lifted. There were tears streaming down his cheeks and, as I looked into his eyes, I saw love and joy. He quietly reached up and took the water.

"Even though I was only twelve then, I can still remember vividly the feeling I had as I watched this rugged old man partake of the sacrament. I knew, without a doubt, that he was feeling something about the sacrament that I had never felt. I determined then that I wanted to feel those same feelings." (Author unknown.)

And Dallas always emphasized that when we love, we will serve. In his pocket, he carried a replica of the tiny widow's mite of the Savior's story which he often used to demonstrate that it is the serving that matters, not the size or quantity or visibility of such service. "All the animals were so happy in the beautiful green forest. The elephants played in the river. Giraffes ate from the tall trees. Monkeys hung from vines, chattering. Lions and tigers rolled around in the underbrush.

Multicolored birds flitted about, looping through the air and perching on tree limbs and branches. Hummingbirds drank nectar from the garden of pastel flowers. The animals had a wonderful life. They loved their forest.

"One day, suddenly, hot tendrils of flaming fire began to lick at the beautiful forest greenery. Higher and more ferocious grew the flames, chasing the animals from their home. From all parts of the forest the animals raced to the river, just ahead of the deadly menace. In their haste, no one saw the hummingbird, its tiny wings fluttering hundreds of times a minute. It flew to the river, scooped up a beak full of water, and returned hastily to dump it on the rapidly approaching flames. Over and over again, the hummingbird repeated the sequence.

"Finally an elephant paused to watch, eventually asking: 'Little bird, what are you doing?'

"'I'm getting water to put out the fire,' replied the hummingbird.

"'But,' retorted the elephant, 'surely you don't think that you can stop the fire!'—to which the hummingbird sweetly replied: 'Perhaps not, but I love the forest and I am doing my part to save it.'"

Though Dallas was a great story teller, he seldom shared his own heart-felt stories about love. Some of them were just too personal, too private, too profound to present in public.

When Dallas was young he, like most young men in the Rocky Mountains, went hunting. He had a treasured rifle or two and was always ready for a little wilderness stalking.

But then, at an October general conference in the mid-1970's, things began to change. President Spencer W. Kimball gave a discourse in Priesthood meeting emphasizing care in hunting attitudes and behaviors which Dallas ever after called the "Don't Shoot the Little Birds Speech." President Kimball's words touched Dallas deeply. He sold his rifles deciding that, in this day and age, hunting was not an activity in which he needed to be involved. He was pragmatic, however. If necessary for food, he would have procured a rifle or bow and arrow and gone to the forest.

Dallas never talked to me further about this decision, and I'm sure he would have said it was not a decision others needed to make. But he felt strongly that it was something he should do. Perhaps, for him, it softened and mellowed his heart with regard to our Father's creations and taught him of sensitivity and love. Even when fishing, he would most often catch and release.

At The Ranch in Brazil he cared, tenderly, for the bees, rabbits, horses and other life forms. When some of the rabbits died of an unexplained disease, he buried them quietly and sadly. He learned to tolerate and finally to love our pesky family dog, Bitsy. He admired the amazing animals in Africa. I guess I knew he was affectionately connected to God's creations and gradually becoming more so, but didn't realize how deep his feelings were until one fall day in Utah during another October conference time.

He had gone alone that day to fish in Utah's high Uintah mountains, at his favorite Butterfly Lake. He stayed to enjoy the evening fishing; and, when it was almost dark, he packed his gear in the car and started down the mountain.

Not too far from the lake, however, he approached a car parked in the road at an awkward angle. The driver waved him down. Dallas stopped to investigate and discovered that the man had hit a deer, a small doe, on the dark mountain highway. The car was damaged but in working order. The deer was alive, but severely injured and suffering. The driver of the car had no weapon to bring the suffering of the deer to a tragic but needed end. He was hoping someone coming down the road would.

Dallas, unfortunately, had only the knife he used to clean fish. They waited a few minutes. No other cars came by. There seemed to be no alternative. Dallas went to get the knife.

Back at our hotel room in Salt Lake, he spent most of that night sitting in a chair, awake. When I asked him if something was the matter, he told me about the deer. The room was dark, but I knew there were tears. And I knew that was not the only night he spent awake, thinking about the events on the mountain road, haunted by life and death and beauty.

He never told me any more about the pain and love that experience created in his heart. He didn't need to.

The Greatest Gift
    by Dallas N. Archibald (First published in *Christmas Treasures, Stories and Reminiscences from General Authorities*, Deseret Book Company, Salt Lake City, Utah; 1994, 27-29). When Dallas was asked to submit a Christmas experience or story for a book that would be a compilation of such writings from various general authorities, he first searched his memory for a meaningful personal experience. Unable to recall anything of universal significance, he composed a short story filled with some of the things he loved most: scriptures, missionary work, family, and pine trees.

The cold, brisk morning air of winter instantly turned Ron's breath into a small cloud of vapor and made his skin tingle. He'd left his coat inside when he stepped onto the back porch of his home. For a few minutes he wanted to be by himself and think, and the change from the warmth of the house to the crisp, frosty air outside was invigorating.

Dawn was just beginning to break and he could see, silhouetted by the light on the horizon, the dark shapes of the pine trees along the back fence. His friends and neighbors continually kidded him about his devotion to those trees, and always he explained that these weren't ordinary pine trees. They were Christmas trees, homegrown, and with an eternal purpose.

His only child, Nancy, had been born on the tenth of December, just fifteen days before Christmas. Early the next spring, as soon as the ground thawed, Ron planted a small blue spruce in the far corner of the back yard beside the fence. Before that, though, he had done some research, talking with forestry experts and even making a special trip to a nearby university. It was with this newly obtained knowledge that he selected the blue spruce which, in accordance with the climatic conditions of his area, would be the right size for a Christmas tree in a little less than eight years.

Armed with soil test kits, proper nutrients, equipment for shaping and, most important, a theme from the scriptures, he had put in the first tree. And each year afterward for six years another seedling had been planted. In this way, Ron had initiated his own special Christmas tradition.

On Nancy's eighth birthday, Ron took the afternoon off from work and went home early. Bundled up in winter clothes he, his wife, Mary, and Nancy had gone to the back yard. There, as a family, they had cut down the first of the seven trees planted in an evenly spaced row along the fence. They cut the tree just above the bottom few branches because, Ron explained, one of these branches would curl up toward the sun; seven years later, when Nancy turned fifteen, it would be the Christmas tree for that year.

Both Ron and Mary knew that children, like pine trees, need proper soil, proper nutrients, and proper shaping both spiritually and temporally. This was one of those shaping, teaching times—an especially important one, as Nancy was preparing to be baptized. Ron felt a ruffle of excitement inside. He'd waited eight years for this day.

After the tree had been secured in its stand and placed in its holiday location in the living room, Ron began. "Nancy, stand back and tell me what you see."

With a squeal of delight and youthful joy she replied immediately, "A pretty tree, Daddy."

"And what did Father Lehi see first in his dream?" She thought for a moment this time before answering, "A pretty tree."

"Go and get the Book of Mormon from the bookshelf," he suggested, "and as we decorate the tree let's see what comparisons we can make."

As the family took turns reading chapter eleven of First Nephi, Ron pointed out that Nephi, through the assistance of the Spirit, had seen the Christmas story in a vision. Nephi wanted to see the same things his father, Lehi, had seen in the dream, and an angel had opened the understanding of heaven to him. After he was shown the tree his father had seen, Nephi expressed a desire to know the interpretation of this vision. In response, he had been taught of the Savior. The angel then asked Nephi if he now knew the meaning of his father's dream, and Nephi answered, "Yea, it is the love of God." Years later another disciple of Jesus Christ, John, would say, "For God so loved the world, that he gave his only begotten Son." (John 3:16.) The love of God for us is represented in His Son, Jesus Christ, Ron explained.

The rod of iron, which is the word of God as contained in the holy scriptures, and also the words of the living servants of God on this earth, will lead us to the fountain of living waters, or to the tree of life, which represent the love of God. Jeremiah was told that the Lord is the fountain of living waters. (Jeremiah 2:13.) The fountain of living waters, the tree of life, and the love of God are all symbolic of Jesus Christ. Later, when Nephi was instructing his brothers, he told them that the tree of life and its precious fruit, "is the greatest of all the gifts of God." (1 Nephi 15:36.)

After this discussion, Mary gave Nancy a set of scriptures and a picture of the prophet to put beneath the tree. In this way they would be reminded that these are the iron rod that leads to the tree of life—the Savior. Ron explained that the green of the tree represented the hope of eternal life, hope that comes from the Savior and his atonement.

As the family strung the multicolored lights through the tree branches, Ron spoke of the light of Christ. Everyone has it to bring them to the truth, he said, but after her baptism, Nancy would enjoy an increase of that light. By the laying on of hands she would receive the gift of the Holy Ghost; then, as long as she was worthy, the Spirit would be her constant companion to protect her, to guide her and to testify to her of Jesus Christ.

When Ron and Mary, with Nancy's help, hung round, red ornaments on the tree, Ron talked about the blood of Christ which was shed for our sins so that we through our faithfulness could be cleansed and purified and one day return to the presence of God and have eternal life. The red ornaments on their tree were a symbol of the atonement.

Although there would be angels and stars in other Christmas decorations in their home, the top of their tree would display something different. That last adornment was a beautiful red bow with flowing tails of red ribbon. Through this they would remember that the tree of life, the Savior, and his atonement are the greatest of all gifts.

That first year, the decorated Christmas tree was like an invitation to have the Savior in their home, and in the comfort of its soft colored lights the family spent many special moments discussing Nancy's baptism, which took place the first Saturday in January.

The next day, for the first time as an official member of the Church, Nancy partook of the sacrament in remembrance of the Savior and his sacrifice. Monday night in family home evening, the family dismantled their "tree of life" and put the decorations away until the next December 10.

Through the years thereafter, Ron found great solace in the row of seven pine trees, each in a different stage of growth. In moments of challenge and of joy, he received spiritual encouragement from them. He worked to nurture and shape the trees knowing that each one, year after year, would play an important role in bringing thoughts of the Savior and his atonement into Christmas.

The morning light was brighter now and the snowy yard glistened. Ron had stayed on the porch longer than planned. Today, later in the afternoon, Nancy would be home from her college classes. The three of them, he and Mary and Nancy, would be together once again. He looked toward the fence. The tallest of the pine trees this year was the last one in the row. Almost twenty-one years had passed since he had planted the first. From that planting he had gained another cutting by re-directing a lower branch. Seven years ago he had torn up that stump and had planted a new tree in its place. Now it was time to cut the last of the original seven, and next spring a new seedling would be planted in its spot.

Over the years, Ron and Mary had sought the guidance of the Spirit, praying that their shaping and nurturing would give Nancy the proper direction in her life to bring her to an active knowledge of the Savior in applying his teachings. This evening they would again decorate a tree and review the account of Nephi. And again, as when she was eight, the discussions would be in anticipation of an event which was soon to be. Her mission application papers had been forwarded to Salt Lake City by the stake president and hopefully, before the first Saturday of the new year, she would receive her call from the prophet of the Lord to go and teach others of the tree of life and its precious fruit.

The winter air suddenly made Ron shiver. He turned and opened the door. It was time to go to work, but he would be back home a little early today. It was Nancy's birthday—time to begin Christmas again.

Primary Care

When, at April General Conference in 1997, Dallas was re-assigned from area president of Brazil to area president of Chile, we began to pack and look ahead to new responsibilities and challenges with the mixed emotions which always accompany departures and arrivals. Leaving Brazil was difficult, as much for the accumulation of almost fifteen years of clutter in the closets as for the inevitable emotions. The trip itself, however, was relatively easy. Even though our plane was delayed some six hours at the São Paulo airport because of mechanical problems, by nightfall we had soared high over the Andes and landed in Santiago.

I, very quickly, began the task of settling into the apartment and polishing up some very rusty Spanish. Teresa, having opted to go to Chile with us for a few months rather than to college in the United States, enrolled in Spanish classes. Dallas began transferring, through teaching and training, all the ideas and programs that had worked so well in Brazil, for example: the Young Women's camp program, a stronger focus on spirituality for Young Men, methods for missionaries to have more success in teaching fathers and families, and increased temple attendance.

At the same time he, as always, immersed himself in the culture. During the years in Brazil, he always had a slight Spanish accent on his Portuguese (people would often ask if he was from Argentina). Now, in Chile, he had a Portuguese accent on his Spanish with the two languages living in less than peaceful co-existence with each other. But he was never one to let mortal shortcomings and academic errors restrain him. He just plowed ahead, learning as he went, assuming that others would ask if they didn't understand.

Following a pattern he established in Brazil, one of the first things he did in Chile was request a copy of Chile's national anthem as well as a copy of the more popular national song of the heart, "*Si Vas Para Chile*" (If You Go to Chile) He learned to sing both songs and then, in every missionary meeting, he taught them to all the foreign elders and sisters so they could join the Chileans in a chorus of national culture and pride. Soon, as expected, the Chilean people began to believe that he was one of them.

A few months into our assignment in Santiago, Sister Sharon Taylor, the wife of Dallas's first counselor, Elder Jerald L. Taylor, mentioned that she had noticed a particular weakness in the Primary organization in Chile. With so many new converts, the members really did not understand how to use the Primary program as a method to teach children the gospel rather than as just a simple nursery. Dallas pondered the problem and then, with his counselors, decided to proceed with a training program initially for the forty-eight stakes in and near Santiago.

The Area Presidency requested for us, their wives, to plan a possible method and structure for the training sessions. We put together some ideas, based on a similar program that had been effective in Brazil, and submitted them to the Area Presidency. They made suggestions and we counseled together, finally developing an evening of training about which all of us felt very excited. After we refined the program, the Area Presidency called several Chilean sisters to present the material.

The forty-eight stakes would be divided into four groups of twelve stakes each, and the program would be presented on four sequential Friday nights. It would begin with a session that would include a couple of short discourses from priesthood leaders and a couple of testimonies regarding children and Primary. A stake president, who was the husband of one of the Chilean sisters presenting the material, had seen the potential of the Primary through new eyes after helping his wife with her portion of the program. He willingly gave a short discourse and testimony.

After the general session, the large group was split into five smaller groups determined by colored stickers received as the participants entered the building. Each small group then visited five classrooms where different aspects of Primary were demonstrated. Those with red stickers began with sharing time, then moved to music, lessons, reverence, and leadership. The other colors went in a different order until everyone had received the training in each room.

As the speakers and teachers moved effectively through the first evening of training, they became more and more excited as their students (the priesthood and Primary leaders in attendance) caught the vision and the enthusiasm. The area presidency and their wives, having listened to all the training presentations during a dress rehearsal, wandered the halls seeing that no one was lost or left out and being certain that everyone found their way to the correct next location during the classroom transfer which took place every fifteen minutes.

On the third Friday of presentations, Dallas happened to check the parking lot during one of his wanderings. There he found a less active member, Juan Andrés Zúñiga, the brother of the president of a stake located some two hours from Santiago. Brother Zúñiga didn't attend church, but was always willing to help with transportation when the stake needed assistance.

Dallas stepped outside to talk to him and after a minute of chit-chat invited him to attend the training meetings. Brother Zúñiga declined, but Dallas was never one to take "no" for a final answer. He explained what was happening inside and that it was not a regular church meeting. He said it would be easy to slip into a couple of the rooms, unnoticed, and enjoy the fun. Brother Zúñiga began to soften a bit and Dallas gradually moved him closer and closer to the entrance of the building. Dallas told him he could leave at any time and said he would be in the hall waiting to talk to him about any subject matter.

Since it sounded like a no-lose situation, Brother Zúñiga entered his first Primary presentation to learn about Primary music. Fifteen minutes later, as everyone was moving on to the next location, he passed Dallas in the hall so excited and in such a hurry to get to the next room that he was barely coherent. Every fifteen minutes, he rushed back through the hallway, asking directions to the next room, his enthusiasm ever growing.

By the time the evening was over, he was prepared to return to church the next Sunday with the hope that they would give him a calling in Primary.

A few weeks later Dallas received a letter from Juan's brother, the stake president:

"Dear Elder Archibald,

"I am very thankful to be able to greet you and express my gratitude and joy for the things you do in this wonderful work.

"Perhaps you will remember that on March 13 of this year, you became a special guide and teacher for my brother, Juan Andrés, who at that time traveled with us in order to drive some of our dear sisters to the special Primary training meeting.

"I was so happy when I realized that my brother was participating in the classes in the same group I was in. I asked him who had invited him to participate and he said to me, in an affectionate tone, 'some foreigner outside.'

"After the meeting, I saw you speaking enthusiastically with Juan about fishing for trout in the valley where we live.

"This past Sunday, I…had some business to take care of in the ward to which my brother belongs, and how great was my joy again to see him come to the chapel dressed in his best suit with his beautiful family.

"I wanted you to know that he was well received by the elder's quorum president and was invited to have an interview with the bishop who later told me that Juan has a goal to go to the temple.

"Thank you for inviting my brother to come unto Christ.

"Your brother in the gospel.

Vicente Zúñiga Figueroa

Los Andes, Chile"

That experience with the Primary meetings and Juan Andrés was so intertwined with the priorities in Dallas's life—missionary work, temple work, strengthening the saints, and loving the children—that they may have combined to be the highlight of the year; a year that would end on December 14 at the Bio Bio River.

Lead me, Guide me, Walk beside me
Help me find the way
Teach me all that I must do
To live with him someday.

BEHOLD, I WILL SEND FOR MANY FISHERS...
(Jeremiah 16:16)

In the spring of 1997, Teresa was living in the United States. One night she had a dream. Though she didn't recognize her surroundings in the dream, she knew she was at home. The doorbell rang and she answered the door. The face of the man standing there was unclear, but he spoke to her as if he knew her: "Your father was away on a trip and there has been an accident. Your mother has been trying to reach you. You need to call her now." She awoke from that dream crying and called me in Brazil to say how real the dream had seemed.

On the night of December 14, 1998, her bishop rang the doorbell of the apartment where she had been living for less than a year. "Your father was away on a trip and there has been an accident," he said. "Your mother has been trying to reach you. You need to call her now."

Her dream was only the first of other warnings.

On December 2, 1998, I went to the Santiago Temple alone with several personal concerns on my mind. I was seeking confirmation that my current plans of action were approved of by the Lord. If I received no contrary impressions or course corrections, I would know that I just needed patience in order for the plans to work out. I had used that method successfully before in other situations.

Pondering, meditating, I waited for a while after the session before returning to the locker room to change from my white temple clothes to my regular street clothes. I received no impressions, no instructions to follow any other routes. Finally feeling that the issues and plans were in order, I went to change. However, as I closed the door to my locker I was enveloped in a cocoon seemingly made of rays of light, and powerful waves of emotion swept over me as I saw clearly written across my mind the words: "Everything's going to be okay." I found breathing difficult, and my tears fell in rivers. I did not understand why I was receiving such comprehensive confirmation that my life—all of it, it seemed, not just the current questions—was going to be okay. I had been at peace with the issues on my mind. Seconds passed. Ten. Fifteen. Twenty. The power began to subside. Still my tears fell, and my solitary tissue was drenched. I was grateful that the Spirit had chosen this very private moment to speak to me—though I knew not why.

At the time of this experience, Dallas was traveling on a mission tour in southern Chile. When he returned on December 9, I told him what had happened. He asked only one question: "How do you feel about things now?" I replied, "I am at peace."

Dallas left again on December 12 for his last stake conference of 1998. I drove him to the airport so I would have the car to finish some last minute Christmas errands. We were planning to spend the holidays with the family in the United States that year. He had his small briefcase filled with all he needed for the meetings and a large green duffle packed with fishing equipment for Monday's trip to the Bio Bio.

"Our last meeting Sunday night," he had told me with a sheepish grin unsuccessfully camouflaging boyish excitement, "is up in the mountains. President Broadbent and I thought we would check out a river Monday morning."

There was so much to do before we left for Utah on Wednesday that I wanted to plead for his return, but I just couldn't. When his call to the

First Quorum of the Seventy in 1996 nullified his long-standing plans for early retirement, he declared with some determination and a twinkle in his eyes: "I will still take retirement—one day at a time every Monday." An occasional mission tour or other responsibility sometimes took him away from his out-of-doors wonderland; but first in Brazil and then in Chile, on Mondays he found some place to throw in a line with a hook on the end, to relax and let time pass without ever looking at a clock.

That December 12 at the Santiago airport, he unloaded his gear as I slipped into the driver's seat and turned to wave to him over my shoulder. He gave me the thumb's up sign, signifying "Hold down the fort. I'll be back soon." As I drove away, I saw him through the rear view mirror still standing there, watching me. Then he turned and lugged the green duffle through the door of the airport.

Sunday night he called to say the meetings had gone well. He was ready for a fishing trip and a plane trip to Utah. Teresa had called earlier wanting to talk with him, share some news and some ideas. I asked her if she wanted him to try and reach her later from his hotel, or if she wanted to call again late Monday night after he came home. "No," she said. "I think I'll just wait until Thursday when you're here in Salt Lake."

Teresa's dream and my emotional experience in the Santiago Temple were not the only warnings. Dallas had not mentioned his impressions to me, but I would learn later that he had mentioned them to others.

"I don't feel like I'm ready to leave Chile yet," he told the Broadbents, "but I have the strongest impression that I'm going to receive a change of assignment." And another friend, Roger Howard, who visited us in Santiago at the end of November told me later that Dallas had commented to him, "I'm sorry I won't be around to see all the good things which will be happening with the Church in Chile."

Roger asked why he would not be around since he had only been in Chile a year-and-a-half, to which Dallas replied, "I don't know. I only know that I will be leaving Chile soon."

He did not share these impressions with me except for an occasional "I don't want to leave Chile yet," to which I always replied, "Maybe we won't be transferred this year." I imagine that he did not mention them to me because I would have wanted to discuss and dissect them and there was nothing to discuss or dissect. He only knew what he was feeling, no facts, no details.

Elder Jerald Taylor, Dallas's first counselor in the Chile Area Presidency, rang my doorbell December 14 in the early afternoon. I couldn't absorb what he said: "Dallas has disappeared at the river. They can't find him." I thought there must be some misunderstanding. I expected him to call from somewhere in Chile at any moment.

But the hours ticked by and there was no phone call. By nightfall, the search efforts were on the Chilean news and from there moving around the world. With the help of Elder and Sister Taylor and the Church operators in Salt Lake City, I notified family members in the United States. Once that unpleasant task was accomplished I advised my liaison, Elder Russell M. Nelson of the Quorum of the Twelve, that everyone had been contacted. The public communications department of the Church was then free to release any information and bulletins.

Monday night was long and sleepless. Tuesday ticked by. I received a package from Dallas that day, delivered by Elder Taylor: two beautiful black linen sweaters from southern Chile. They were to have been my Christmas present, originally intended to be stored at the office until our departure for Utah.

I found I had acquired a kind of hyperactivity, unable to stay in one place or concentrate on any one thing for very long, yet without enough physical energy to accomplish much more than take our little fox terrier, Bitsy, for walks.

Phone calls began coming in from around the world. I fielded them all and assured everyone that everything possible was being done. The Chilean search and rescue teams were excellent and were only being hampered by the multitude of church members and missionaries who had attended the weekend conference sessions and flocked to the river to see if they could help.

Teresa called at midnight. She was at her grandmother's house and had been reading her father's conference talk about children in the November 1992 Ensign. Suddenly she felt overcome with emotion accompanied by a calm reassurance which clearly stated, "Everything's going to be okay." When she repeated the same words to me that I had seen printed in my mind almost two weeks earlier at the temple, I knew that whatever the outcome, it was in the Lord's hands and it would definitely be okay. I did not know the outcome or what okay meant, but I was at peace.

I spent an hour on the phone with President Broadbent going over the details of the events at the river. He was baffled by the circumstances, unable to give any explanation for what had occurred. I sensed that I was more at peace than he was.

Wednesday and Friday mornings, President Robert Wells at the Santiago Temple allowed me to have a few minutes alone in the Celestial Room during a very quiet time at the temple. The peace continued and there were no messages.

Back at our apartment, I added legal and financial papers to the stack of things I had gathered to take to Utah for Christmas. When Dallas was still missing on Wednesday, I decided to delay the trip for two days. I would leave for the United States on Friday night, December 18, with or without news. Thursday passed quietly. My first tears of the week came as the plane lifted off Chilean soil. I couldn't really focus on the continuing search in southern Chile. I only knew that I wasn't supposed to be making this trip alone.

As I stepped off the plane in Salt Lake City welcomed by church leaders and family, my thoughts were mostly with Teresa. Though I still held out a small shaft of hope, I knew how much she would miss her Dad: her playmate, her idol, the wind beneath her wings.

I made the effort to unpack, clean up, and visit some friends who were only in town for the day. On Sunday morning, Teresa and I attended church. When we returned home, a message to call Elder Nelson was on the answering machine. The search was over. Hope of finding him alive was gone. His body had been found floating on the surface of the river not far from where he was last seen. In that moment, the lights in my life went out. Teresa, very quickly, turned them on again.

"Mom, do you realize Dad made it! He's there! He's busy and happy. We need to be happy, too."

She was right. I reached for the sunshine and found it. Still, I let her make the calls to notify the family.

Dallas was not found by the rescue team. Rather, a passerby saw his body floating on the surface and notified the searchers. I was told by one who was there that it was good that the discovery happened this way. The rescue team had become very close, had some spiritual discussions and experiences together. It was best that an outsider made the discovery, and the team then went together, united, to make the recovery.

Of course it was good, I thought. Everything about the events was under the Lord's direction.

I met with family members Sunday and Monday to explain the spiritual experiences Teresa and I had, hoping to pass on some of our peace.

Christmas Week: With the brethren in Salt Lake City we planned the funeral which would be under the direction of the First Presidency. With the leaders in Chile, we coordinated the shipment of the body requesting that a Brazilian flag and a Chilean flag be placed inside the casket. With the help of the Spirit, I found the right legal and financial advisors to put the temporal matters in their proper places. I worked hard, but since my hyperactivity had accelerated, it was easy.

The casket arrived at the Salt Lake City airport on Christmas Eve. We concluded all preparations for Monday's funeral on Saturday, December 26.

Sunday night, December 27, Teresa drove me to the mortuary for a few moments alone. I felt like it was the first time I had stopped moving since I left Santiago over a week before. As we turned into the parking lot, dramatic music emanated from the radio and the words seemed to flow directly from my heart: "And I will always love you." After a trying but rarely emotional week, now I was unable to stay the tears. I had been so busy yet so at peace that it took outside influences to bring my feelings to the surface.

As I sat alone next to the closed casket with its decorative spray of yellow flowers, I talked and I thought and I asked questions and I hoped that Dallas was near. I knew not what the future might bring; nevertheless, light from his life lit up the uncertain path ahead. I vowed to let his love and service, his humor and optimism, his conviction that anything is possible be my guide.

TRIBUTES

The doors to the Eagle Gate Stake Center in Salt Lake City opened at 8 a.m. on Monday, December 28, 1998, so we would have time to greet friends and family before the 10 a.m. funeral. Surprisingly, the line soon drifted out the door and down the street. We had not known how many to expect. After all, Dallas and I had been overseas for so many years. With the extended family, I greeted as many guests as possible; but by 9:15 a.m. it was obvious that the line was growing not diminishing. I began walking down the hall, briefly speaking to as many as I could until we were notified that there was no more time.

After the family prayer was offered by my cousin, Richard Reed, we all followed the casket into the chapel. Every seat from the pulpit to the stage was occupied. I saw Bryce and Anna-Marie, Jeff and Barbara, so many friends, so many missionaries, so many Brazilians. The First Presidency and most of the apostles were seated on the stand with many other general authorities on the right side of the congregation. In such company perhaps I should have felt nervous or awed or sad or afraid, but I did not. Though some might suggest that I was suffering from the effects of shock, all I know is that I felt an extra measure of true gratitude and peace.

For this formal service presided over by the First Presidency, Teresa and I had asked for and were each given permission to give a personal tribute. After the opening song, "Called to Serve"—which I had sung so often in missionary meetings while standing at Dallas's side—and the prayer by Dallas's former bishop, Keith W. Wilcox, it was my turn.

"It is wonderful to see so many family members, friends, and missionaries—some from so far away. Occasions when we can get together are always special, no matter the circumstances.

"Dallas loved people. He would have loved to visit with all of you today, to share some of his enthusiasm, optimism, and vision. He would want us to hold on to those attributes now, attributes he saw as manifestations of the principle of hope. He always had hope that everything would work out okay.

"When we first met, Dallas was a very recently returned missionary from Uruguay and I often accompanied him on assignments to speak in various sacrament meetings. At that time, he always used a particular scripture as the basis for his remarks. I heard him use it again just a few weeks ago. He said it was, for some reason, his favorite.

"'Oh that I were an angel, and could have the wish of mine heart, that I might go forth and speak with the trump of God, with a voice to shake the earth, and cry repentance unto every people!

"Yea, I would declare unto every soul, as with the voice of thunder, repentance and the plan of redemption, that they should repent and come unto our God, that there might not be more sorrow upon all the face of the earth.

"But behold, I am a man, and do sin in my wish; for I ought to be content with the things which the Lord hath allotted unto me' *(Alma 29:1-3).*

"When using this scripture, Dallas would always point out that because Alma did in fact do the work the Lord had given him, the

164

desires of his heart were granted. Alma now speaks with the trump of God from the pages of The Book of Mormon. Elder Archibald, likewise, was willing to do whatever work the Lord gave him. So, perhaps, he like Alma can now receive the desires of his heart and in some way teach the principles of the gospel he loved with even more power.

"Dallas had unique gifts of leadership which I know were particularly valuable to the work. He would still be with us if those unique gifts were not needed elsewhere for some special purpose.

Called to serve Him, Heavenly King of glory,
Chosen e'er to witness for His name.
Far and wide we tell a Father's story,
Far and wide His love proclaim.
(Hymns, 249)

"Dallas spent his life serving far and wide. He is now serving in one more distant land. When we moved to Chile in 1997 after living for fifteen years in Brazil, we were often asked if we missed Brazil. Dallas always responded, with a sense of urgency and a twinkle in his eye: 'I haven't had time and, besides, the work is the same.' I'm sure he would say something similar about his current change of assignment.

"From November 28 until December 14 when the accident in Chile occurred, Dallas and I had been together only a few hours on three separate days as he had been away from home on assignments. Now he is on an even more extended tour of duty; but I know that in the perspective of eternity, it won't be long until we are together again.

"I testify of the truth of the Gospel of Jesus Christ as found in the Church of Jesus Christ of Latter-day Saints. I am grateful, beyond words, for the mission of Jesus Christ and the ordinances of His Gospel which promise that we can be together forever someday."

Then Teresa looked at Dallas's life from a different perspective.

"My mother has just spoken of the spirituality and faith of my father, of the great leader and servant of the gospel that he was. I would like to share with you the lighter, fun-loving side of my father which was characteristic of him, and which all of you have been a part of. These memories are ones that were great fun yet the lessons that I learned from him were most important for laying down the foundation of who I am and who I will become.

"My father had a lust of life. He always had a knack for turning everything into an absolutely wonderful, beautiful thing. He loved to shop for others and delighted in surprising others. I have many tangible memories of my father through the objects that he bought for me. He loved to eat and visit. I have many fond memories of dinners out with my parents and their friends. He loved nature. We had a ranch in Brazil that he adored. Fishing, skiing, jet-skis, sailing, and cars were a few of his passions. He even loved animals. After thirteen years he found a special place in his heart for a very special family member: our dog, Bitsy. Music also touched a chord with him. I remember riding around in the car with him as he blasted opera or big band from the stereo while directing the music and singing at the top of his lungs.

"There was a determination in him that was tempered by love and patience. When I was in 9th grade, he was the coach of a softball team I was on. One of my favorite memories of those games was that he would have his assistant coach direct the team while he would help the players who needed to brush up their skills. After one particular game, I can't remember if we won or lost, but I remember that my Dad presented us with heart necklaces to show us how much we meant to him as a team. A few years ago, I received a call from a friend who was on the team and she said that she still had the heart and it reminded her of how much the team members meant to my father.

"He loved to teach the gospel. I remember going on mission tours with him and as he would teach the missionaries, he would shout and *pound the podium. He would come alive when sharing the gospel with missionaries. Then afterwards, he would receive letters and comments that he would share with my mother and myself. I remember that there would be a softer appearance about him as he read those letters. That was when he learned from those missionaries and his next teaching came from the feedback of people he taught.*

"Another part of his teaching and learning was through children that he met in his life. He eagerly looked forward to the privilege of teaching a child and even greater than teaching was the privilege of learning from a child. My cousin, Russell, who is twelve years old puts it more eloquently than I ever could. A few days after my father had been missing, I was over with some of my family playing with some of their newborn guinea pigs. I went to walk out the door when Russell said something that made me realize the effect my father had. He said, "I'm going to cut out a picture from a newspaper clipping and frame it and put it by my bed so that I will always remember how special he was to me." My father would be elated to know that someone he loved would remember him in such a way.

"From that love of children came his love of family, both extended and immediate. One of the greatest examples he gave me of that love was for my mother. He would tease her constantly. I remember he would always play practical jokes on her and frustrate her at the dinner table with his comments, but it was from those things that I realized he loved her more than everything in the world.

"If there was one word I would use to describe him, it would be 'committed'—committed to his faith, to enjoying life, to his friends, and to his family. In my heart this is what makes a great man. My father had achieved that in his life. As we say farewell to him in this life, may we remember him for those memories and qualities. Then his legacy will live on in us."

The balance of the meeting belonged to the brethren, Dallas's associates in church service. President Joe J. Christensen, of the Presidency of the Seventy, conducted. All the speakers emphasized the abiding faith, hope, and charity that belonged to Elder Dallas Nielsen Archibald.

President Harold G. Hillam, of the presidency of the Seventy: *"I always found him to be absolutely fair. I never heard him say a negative word about a person, not ever. He was always kind... Elder Archibald loved people, he loved nature and he loved life, but he didn't love any of them as much as he loved his Heavenly Father and his Savior, Jesus Christ."*

Elder Richard G. Scott, of the Quorum of Twelve Apostles: *"I speak for the thousands of individuals around the world who loved Dallas, loved his service, appreciate his devotion. I first met Dallas as our bishop in Mexico City when he cared for our family... In these other assignments that he's fulfilled so well and have been mentioned, I've grown to love and respect him. But I want to talk about what, for me, is more important...the role of husband and father. He's been a lot of fun and a great person to be with. He's also been very caring and tender."*

President James E. Faust, second counselor in the First Presidency: *"Dallas Archibald was both righteous and favored. We are all shocked by his sudden passing. Of course we grieve. Of course we mourn. But I should like to look on the positive side of his life. We recall a life of service... the tremendous good that he accomplished, the greatness of his life, and the homes that have been blessed by his ministry. He's done so many things, brought to pass so much righteousness, particularly among the Latin people who love him and whom he loved so very much."*

President Thomas S. Monson, first counselor in the first Presidency: *"When I think of his virtues I'm impressed by the statement of the Lord concerning Nathanael, whom He saw in the distance, and said, 'Behold, an Israelite indeed, in whom is no guile!' (John 1:47.) Dallas Archibald was a man with no chink in his armor, no guile in his soul, no flaw in his character. There wasn't room, because love was so dominant in his heart."*

And the Prophet and President of the Church, Gordon B. Hinckley: *"He was a remarkable man, there's no question about it... Nobody can tell the consequences of that which he has done; a baptism here, a teaching of the truth there will go on bearing fruit for generations yet to come...*

"He's gone. None of us can understand why, but we know that there is Someone who does understand why, and that there's a purpose in all of this... His capacity to teach the gospel here will be magnified in the area to which he has gone..."

(Comments of the First Presidency previously published in the *Ensign* magazine; © by Intellectual Reserve, Inc.; March 1999; 74; used by permission.)

Dallas would have been humbled and honored by the tributes and expressions of respect and friendship.

Dallas's favorite hymn, "How Great Thou Art," closed the meeting: *"When Christ shall come, with shout of acclamation, and take me home, what joy shall fill my heart! Then I shall bow, in humble adoration and there proclaim, 'My God how great thou art!'"* (Hymns, 86.) During the singing, two Brazilian friends came reverently up the aisle from the back of the crowd carrying a Brazilian flag. They laid the green and yellow banner respectfully next to the yellow flowers on the casket, and white handkerchiefs dabbed at eyes on the stand and throughout the congregation.

Once upon a time, a little boy wished to be a Lamanite. Though the color of his eyes, hair, and skin never changed, he became one with the people of Latin America, with the scriptural tribe of Manasseh. I was certain that, in his new assignment, he was still working with them and for them.

After Elder Helvecio Martins offered the benediction, we filed solemnly out of the chapel. The family filled two limousines which took us to the cemetery for the dedication of the grave. When we arrived at the small private cemetery which was owned by the mortuary in charge of the funeral arrangements, everything was ready. The light brown casket was placed inside a protective concrete vault which would provide support for the walls of the grave.

As those who had come for the dedication escaped the light drizzle of rain by gathering under a green canopy, Dallas's nephew, Niel Archibald, offered the prayer. The mourners were then dismissed, but Teresa and I and a couple of Brazilians lingered.

"How long before they lower the casket?" I asked a representative of the mortuary.

"We usually wait until everyone is gone," he replied. "But, we can do it anytime. Would you like to have it done before you leave?"

I nodded and within two minutes a crew was there to accomplish that final task.

I had not thought to bring a camera. I wish I had, for now there is no way to capture on film the interior lid of the vault. Large letters spelled his name: Elder Dallas Nielsen Archibald—and the dates of his birth and death: July 24, 1938—December 14, 1998. Beside that information, on the left, was carved the outline of a bird, a hummingbird with fluttering wings, drinking nectar from the center of a lovely flower blossom. To me it was the hummingbird in his oft-told tale about the forest fire. Like that little bird, Dallas had always done his part to help, done anything that was asked of him. I knew he was continuing to serve as requested.

I stepped back, ready to leave. The scene was serene: A little snow beneath our feet, a cloudy sky above, a quiet fall of rain, and a magnificent backdrop of nearby Rocky Mountains. Teresa and I had chosen the plot carefully. Dallas would sleep directly under the protective, overhanging branches of an old, stately pine tree. His final resting place. He would have loved it there.

But, in my heart, I knew that my "Energizer Bunny" was not really resting. Not resting at all.

NEW BEGINNINGS

Once the funeral was over, of necessity I turned back to the temporal matters. I finished financial and legal business, confirmed two tickets to Brazil and Chile for Teresa and myself, purchased a car, and went in search of a new residence. I wandered three Utah counties for two days, looking. Because I would be bringing our dog, Bitsy, back with me from Chile, I wanted to settle on something before my return trip to South America.

On the morning of December 31, I was ready to give up the hunt and forfeit my wish when I learned of a townhouse available in the same complex in Salt Lake City where my daughter had been living for a year. I asked to see it and, when I stepped inside, a feeling of peace and comfort told me I had found home. "If I'm not supposed to live here, take this feeling away," I prayed. The feeling increased. Within an hour, I made arrangements with the owner to lease it with an option to buy.

That concluded the business priorities and I felt a need to briefly get away. Jeff and Barbara Marchant in Cedar City, Utah were kind enough to open their doors to me on short notice. There, during the New Year weekend, I found that I felt very much at home in that small southern Utah town. Dallas and I almost always had a get-a-way: the little white camper, Baguio, The Boat, the waterfall at Refugio del Salto, the

Ranch. Cedar City had that "home away from home feeling," and I sensed that it could become my get-a-way. Besides, Dallas and I had seriously considered spending our retirement years in Cedar and I was quite sure that plan would have become a reality. Southern Utah would not be just my retreat. In a way, it was ours.

Back in Salt Lake on January 4, I tied up loose business ends and Teresa and I caught the plane for São Paulo. Although I missed the memorial services held in Dallas's honor in Brazil and Chile, I would have a chance to share my experiences, my testimony, with many people.

Elder Craig Zwick, the Brazil Area President, and his wife, Jan, met us at the São Paulo airport and thereafter anticipated our every need. Dallas and I still had some legal and financial interests in Brazil and the business I had to transact was concluded in record time. I met with friends to share an audio copy of the funeral. I spoke to the employees at the Church offices and tried to pass on faith, hope, and love. Though everyone felt a profound sense of loss, it seemed to me that everyone also felt peace.

Thirty-six hours after arriving in Brazil, Teresa and I were back in the air, on a plane to Chile. Elder and Sister Taylor, who would spend the next four days assisting us in every possible way, met us at the airport and took us home—home to the place where our clothes and books and personal belongings were. There, also, were Dallas's possessions—the green duffle bag which I had last seen through the rear view mirror as he carried it through the door at the Santiago airport, his wallet, his watch, and his ring.

Suddenly, and for the first time, everything was very real. All the prior events—the quiet days waiting for news, the trip to Utah, the legal and financial work, even the funeral and the return to Brazil were preliminary. In Chile, I would face the memories. In Chile, I would say the farewells.

Unlike the atmosphere in Brazil, I sensed that the people in Chile were not yet at peace. These were the people who had lived, first hand, through the December anguish: The loss, the search, the lack of success, the news reports, the discovery, the recovery, the process of sending Dallas's remains to Utah. They had suffered and cried and questioned why, but they had also learned something of faith, faith to accept the Lord's will and confidence that He can do His work in His way.

I met with our American friends and, as they listened to my perspectives and to the audio of the funeral, they wept together and finally closed on their month-long emotional experience. I attended my Santiago ward and shared my testimony of eternal perspectives. I spoke briefly to the employees at the Church offices and told them how much Dallas and I loved Chile and always would.

President Broadbent and his family came to Santiago for an evening while I was there. He had struggled to understand what had happened at the river, questioned if he could have done anything to prevent the outcome. The events, beginning with Dallas's separation from the float tube to his disappearance around the river bend, were so mysterious. And there was also Dallas's comment about feeling certain he would leave Chile soon for a new assignment. President Broadbent gave me some photographs of the river that were taken on December 19, the day before Dallas's body was found, and he told me this story:

"I went to the river several times that week during the search. Elder Taylor came down to Concepción the end of the week, and we drove to the river together. We hiked up on a cliff where we could look down on the river and take these pictures. As we stood there on the cliff, Elder Taylor asked me to point out the place where I last saw Elder Archibald. I gazed for some time at the river. Then, somewhat confused, I turned to Elder Taylor and said, 'I don't know where I last saw

175

him. The bend is not as I remember it. This really doesn't even look like the same river.'"

I had considered traveling to the river, but now I knew there was no need. I scanned the photos. There were no answers at the Bio Bio. Only one thing seemed sure: At the Bio Bio River on December 14, 1998, Dallas was scheduled to leave Chile for a new and, I was certain, singular assignment. I would have to set aside my "What happened?" and "Why?" questions and wait patiently, maybe until eternity, for answers.

When the visits and speaking opportunities in Santiago ended, all that was left for Teresa and me to do was to sort and pack our personal belongings. It was exhausting, sometimes emotional work, but we finished on time. The moving company drove away with our possessions which would be sent by air to Utah. After a couple of nostalgic visits to memorable locations in Santiago, Teresa and I left for the airport with four large suitcases and one small dog.

In Chile I tried to whisper every possible farewell—to people, to places, to the apartment and to the view of the Andes from our window. Nevertheless, departure felt melancholy and out of sequence and the Bio Bio might as well have been in another galaxy. I "closed doors" everywhere, but I did not know how to say goodbye.

One week almost to the minute after landing in São Paulo, Teresa and I touched down back in Salt Lake City. The date was January 13, 1999. "What a difference a month makes," I thought to myself. Dallas taught me to believe in miracles and I was grateful that I had experienced so many during that month, even though none of them was the miracle for which I had hoped.

Now it was really a new beginning for me. I was on my own and so very grateful that he had given me space and let me fly. I promised myself that wherever I went I would do my best to turn life into "a wonderful, beautiful thing." I knew Dallas was living with sunshine, as always. I didn't want to be left behind.

We've always been together though apart,
You're with me every hour of the day.
I hold a prayer for you within my heart,
And we'll go on, with God to light the way.

One day together we will always be—
Sealed for time and all eternity.

Saturday, April 3, 1999. I arrived early for the Saturday morning session of general conference in Salt Lake City and parked in the underground parking lot at the Church Office Building. I was alone, walking through the tunnel under Main Street toward the entrance to the Tabernacle. My mind was wandering, thinking of nothing and everything, of past conferences and this conference. Suddenly there was a vibration in the space around me and a definite awareness that I was not alone.

I wished intently that I could have reached out and held his hand. Instead I only whispered, "I miss you," and blinked away the tears. Ten or fifteen seconds later I knew he was gone.

During the next few days people often asked me if I thought Dallas was at conference. "Yes," I said confidently. "But perhaps he is too busy to stay very long."

I realized that, like me, he was involved in new beginnings.

I Will Always
Love You

Juan Andrés Zúñiga and his family were preparing to be sealed in the Santiago Temple. A little more than a year had passed since the influential Primary training meetings. Elder Taylor called the family to ask if he could perform the sealing in honor of Elder Archibald. All agreed.

On May 21, 1999, the family gathered for their special day at the temple: Juan Andrés; his lovely wife, Mirian; his four children, Andrea, Ángela, Nelson, and Valéria; his brother, the stake president; along with other family members and friends. Elder Taylor reported that the ceremony was emotional and filled with the Spirit—and he told me the rest of the story.

"When we had concluded and everyone was leaving the sealing room, I put my arms around Brother Zúñiga and with emotion in my voice said, 'I know Elder Archibald is pleased with these events today.'

"Brother Zúñiga, radiant, his eyes glistening with tears, replied, 'Oh, didn't you see him? He was here.'"

Listening to Elder Taylor, I could envision the reverent elegance of the sealing room, the peace and joy of the family, the happiness glowing in their faces. And I could see Dallas, dressed in his white suit, adorable yet official, tears in his eyes, love in his heart—observing another "wonderful, beautiful thing" in which he had played a very large part.

I held onto the image, for that is the way I expect he will look the next time I see him. On that day, once again, my heart will skip a beat. I'll get all teary, and he'll snicker at me. But after a hug and a kiss, I'll ask my long-awaited questions: "Why did you have to leave?" and "What happened at the river?"

He'll get a twinkle in his eyes and we'll walk away, hand in hand, perhaps to a quiet place beside a lake or a stream. There he will fill in all the blanks for me.

I see us sitting side by side. I don't know what remarkable information he supplies in answer to my questions, and eventually my vision fades. But I do know that from then on we will take every opportunity to fly together past the second star to the right and go straight on 'til morning!

From then on, it will be Peter Pan and Wendy—forever!

EPILOGUE:
AS TIME GOES BY

Though years pass, people still ask me how I'm doing. The answer is always the same: I'm just fine. His legacy continues to light the way.

I have had to stretch to try and learn to love as unconditionally as he did, but I have made progress.

Occasionally I have had to inch into the rising waters of life, alone, and felt the silt and gravel slip beneath me; but, in reaching for a depth of faith I didn't know existed, I have grasped his vision and eventually arrived safely on the other side.

Sometimes I have told a joke or given a humorous reply in conversation and then marveled at the fact that, in some way, I seem to sound like him.

After hugs and handshakes to friends and children of friends leaving on missions, I've given them copies of *The Potter's Hand* and said, often with a catch in my throat, "This is from Dallas."

Though *Baked Alaska* is a rare commodity at my house these days, I have nevertheless become more persistent, more adventurous, more assertive, more confident, more optimistic, more willing to try and fail and try again—maybe just because I have to, being alone, but sometimes I'm certain he must be close by, still teaching me.

One day I was thinking about how he tried but never really understood my wishes for hearts and flowers, for candlelight and sharing. And a thought came clearly: He understands now. Another time I was pondering how he often asked me for sincere feedback on his spontaneous speeches and other presentations and how I never understood his need because I never used to do anything spontaneously. At those times I couldn't respond appropriately but, since I have had to learn spontaneity, now I can. How wonderful it shall be when we rise above all our mortal limitations.

Numerous inanimate humming birds, our family emblem, decorate the house—their gold and crystal forms a reminder that we can, in some small way, always help to extinguish the forest fires around us.

I try to take flowers to the cemetery often, but that spot of color is mostly for my benefit. I know he is satisfied with the pine tree.

Though the Bio Bio still seems worlds away, I have learned to take time to float down my own kinds of rivers.

I have experienced a few more miracles, common and uncommon.

Life *is* a wonderful, beautiful thing.

The lessons from his life continue.

Elder Dallas N. Archibald

He was a teacher of renown and a powerful motivator.
He changed people's lives.